On the Waters of the World

On the Waters of the World

The story of the Meloon Family

by

Robert G. Flood

MOODY PRESS
CHICAGO

© 1989 by
THE MOODY BIBLE INSTITUTE
OF CHICAGO

Portions of this book were adapted from *Saved from Bankruptcy,* by David and Dorothy Enlow, published by Moody Press in 1975.

Scripture quotations, unless noted otherwise, are taken from *The Living Bible,* © 1971 by Tyndale House Publishers.

The use of selected references from various versions of the Bible in this publication does not necessarily imply publisher endorsement of the versions in their entirety.

Quotations on pages 12, 14, 71, and 72 have been reprinted by courtesy of *Powerboat Magazine.*

ISBN: 0-8024-5937-4

1 2 3 4 5 6 Printing/BC/Year 93 92 91 90 89

Printed in the United States of America

Contents

A Word from the President   9

1. On the Waters of the World   11

   Their boats skim the waves on every continent and pull the world's best water-skiers. Their Christian faith also takes a world view.

2. Storm Boats Cross the Rhine   15

   General Eisenhower wanted 569 assault boats—fast! It was an impossible task, but the firm pulled off what even official Washington later called "the miracle production."

3. The Man Who Invented Waterskiing   23

   Who first discovered how to water-ski, when, where, and how? The sport's earliest pioneer, and how Ralph Samuelson's historic feat turned him to God.

4. From Cypress Gardens to Sea World   31

   Correct Craft helps pioneer Florida's famous Cypress Gardens and years later helps bring crowds to nearby Sea World.

5. Yankee Boatbuilder   37

   New England migrant W. C. Meloon plants a boat firm in Florida. The family struggles through the Depression while three sons learn the business.

6. Silver Dollars   41

   City officials deny the boat company a site near Cape Kennedy—until Walt employs an ingenious plan.

7. One Part Know-How; One Part Faith   45
The company matures and prospers with a
president who knows how to "roll up his sleeves."

8. Government Inspectors   51
When the firm refuses a payoff, inspectors start to
reject boats. The Meloons soon pay a costly price
for their high ethics.

9. The Long Climb Back   57
The Meloons hold on to the company and begin to
pay back their creditors. Years later they move
within $50,000 of total solvency.

10. From the Fish's Mouth   63
From the mouth of a fish in the Sea of Galilee Jesus
produced a coin. From the fish's mouth Correct
Craft comes up with its last $50,000.

11. No Fiberglass Trees   69
When Leo Bentz tries to make a deal, W.C. fumes.
He wants no part of a fiberglass boat and materials
that don't come from the forest.

12. Water-Skiers and God   75
Growing numbers of water-ski enthusiasts, from
world-class professionals to the young beginner,
discover a new dimension to life.

13. The Making of a Magazine   81
The *Correct Craft Tribune* reaches into the vast
boating and water-ski world with news of the
industry and the good news of the gospel.

14. The Ski Nautique and the Family Mystique   87
The Meloon family today—three senior brothers,
the new president, the fourth generation.

15. Earthquakes, Jungle Chiefs, and Fire Canoes   95
The Meloon brothers, Walt and Ralph, roam south
of the border as ambassadors for the gospel. A
former jungle killer from Peru visits the plant.

16. In Europe and the Mideast   103
Ralph travels on international sales trips to
Poland, England, Paris, and Beirut.

17. In Frontier Alaska 111
Ralph Jr. travels through the Chitnook Mountains
to one of Alaska's most unusual villages.

18. In China and the Far East:

Boats Open the Door 119
Correct Craft enters Communist China, a land
once totally closed, and foresees a revolution in the
Philippines.

Appendix A: 127
Correct Craft Corporate Milestones

Appendix B: 130
The Meloon Family Tree

Appendix C: 132
Board of Directors of Correct Craft

A Word from the President

After sixty-two years as a boat manufacturer, the purpose of Correct Craft, Inc., has not changed, neither will it change from that of producing quality recreational boats and servicing our customers at a profit as a means of glorifying God and rendering Him excellent.

Correct Craft has an obligation to its stockholders, customers, suppliers, bankers—and yes—even to the government. Correct Craft also has a commitment to its employees, helping each develop to his full potential in skill, knowledge, creativity, technical know-how, job satisfaction, and quality of life. For the glory of God and to fulfill responsibilities to these key individuals and groups, Correct Craft continually strives to increase its financial base. As an industry trendsetter rather than an imitative follower, Correct Craft will accomplish this mission. The business principles, ethics, and morals of Correct Craft are abided through God's strength and wisdom and enable us to stand strong, unyielding to mediocrity.

One cannot predict the future, but God points the way to success in the Bible with the words "count the cost" (Luke 14:28). We interpret this verse to mean planning. With God's wisdom we can form long-range plans and goals. Not only is it a distinct pleasure to meet and satisfy the recreational needs and wants of people, but also while doing so to please Him who holds the future in His hands.

True, many fine, dedicated employees with great skill and technical knowledge have contributed to the growth and success of Correct Craft. We give the real credit, however, to Him who was rich but became poor, that through His poverty and grace we might become rich in spirit. We owe a debt of gratitude to God and to those men who have gone before us, leaving a shining heritage for those who follow in their footsteps. We give thanks to God for His wisdom and blessings, and we thank our customers for their loyalty.

WALTER N. MELOON

1

On the Waters of the World

Each year millions of television viewers watch the world's top professional water-skiers speed over the waters at Callaway Gardens in central Georgia. It is the annual Masters Water Ski Tournament, indisputably the top event of its kind in the world. The official sponsor each year: Correct Craft of Orlando, Florida, manufacturers of the Ski Nautique, the world's most popular water-ski boat. Shows at nearby Sea World also herald Correct Craft as sponsor. It is the oldest family-owned boatbuilding firm in the United States.

An informal business relationship for more than a half century between the Meloon family, founders of Correct Craft, and Cypress Gardens, one of Florida's top tourist attractions, elevated waterskiing from a provincial novelty for daredevils to a worldwide sport. Today in the United States alone, the sport attracts more than 12 million Americans. A 1954 Correct Craft Atom Skier rests as a centerpiece in the Water Ski Hall of Fame.

Four months after the end of World War II, *National Geographic* carried a photo of assault boats jamming a blocked-off street in front of Correct Craft's plant in South Orlando, Florida.[1] In a remarkable event, these craft, built in less than three weeks, helped General Dwight D. Eisenhower's assault troops bring down Adolph Hitler's armies in the closing days of the war.

1. "Winning the War in Supply," *National Geographic* (December 1945).

National Geographic did not tell the whole story, but behind the drama could be found the unique story of the Meloon family and their Christian faith.

"Today the Meloon/Correct Craft name is known to just about anyone who's interested in water skiing," writes Jim Harmon in *Powerboat* magazine. And although its founder, Walter C. Meloon, is gone, he says, sons Walt and Ralph, and grandson Walter N., now president, "have gone on to create the most widely used, easily recognized and arguably the best water ski tow boat in the history of the sport. In the process," he says, "they have done as much to promote organized water skiing as anyone in the industry.

"And there's another side to the story," Harmon adds. "The strong Christian beliefs which permeate the family's professional as well as personal lives have gained the respect and admiration of their peers. One hears such terms as 'honesty,' 'character' and 'integrity' in descriptions of the Meloons, and quickly learns of their distaste for those more often associated with the business world: 'compromise,' 'deal' and 'shortcut,' among others."[2]

Yet precisely because of their high ethics, the family endured years of operation near bankruptcy and almost lost the company. A simple payoff could have spared them the ordeal. The original 1969 version of this book, titled *Saved from Bankruptcy*, by David and Dorothy Enlow, captured the events to that time. Much more has happened since then—including the thrilling story of how in 1984 they finally paid off their last debt. This book takes the story of Correct Craft and the Meloons into 1988.

Why did God take the company through troubled financial waters, and why did the company survive at all? Even early in the firm's road to recovery, the Meloons

2. Jim Harmon, "The Meloons: Three Parts Know-How, Three Parts Faith,"
   Powerboat, August 1982.

could at least suggest some partial answers. Today the picture is much more clear.

As each year passes, more families facing bankruptcy contact the Meloons for counsel. In some cases, Ralph and Walt have sought out the financially troubled. The recession of 1980, the more recent farming crisis, routine business failures, and the plunge in oil prices all open doors for the Meloons to share the lessons they have learned, to encourage the disheartened, and to pray. No one understands like those who have been through it.

The family's world view may offer another clue to the company's financial recovery. As the senior executives of the company, brothers Ralph and Walt have repeatedly traveled the world: Europe, the Mideast, Asia, Africa, the Far East, and the South Pacific. For years Ralph assisted in international sales. Walt has traveled abroad for as long as thirteen weeks with Evangelist Billy Graham. Together the two brothers have logged hundreds of thousands of miles over the years on behalf of their company and their Lord, meeting leaders of government and, of course, of the ever-broadening water-ski world. Wherever they go, people listen. They have blended both business and the gospel, and the more faithful they are to the latter, they believe, the more their business has true meaning.

God is at work in the world, and readers will see evidence of that as Ralph and Walt take you along in their travels. It was my privilege to travel with Ralph in Europe for two weeks and to see firsthand projects in Alaska and Guatemala initiated and encouraged by the Meloons. In later pages of this book you too will come along with them—into both the jungles and the cities of Latin America. You will join the entourage with Chief Tariri, at one time Peru's most feared headhunter, as he steps into the outside world and picks up a Correct Craft boat in Orlando. You will visit the South Pacific. You will be there as the Meloons encourage the sport of waterskiing in the People's Republic of China. You will catch a glimpse of the dynamic Christian movement in Korea. You will scurry through part of Europe, slip into Poland, and venture into the most dangerous section of Beirut. You will rub shoulders—at least briefly—with the world.

You will also meet some of the world's most talented water-skiers—such as national champion Dave Benzel, barefoot champion John Gillette, master freestyle skier Harold Cole, and former overall world champion Cindy Todd. Active in the water-ski division of the Fellowship of Christian Athletes (FCA), headquartered at the Correct Craft plant in Orlando, they will tell you how their lives were changed, and they will let you in on the spiritual dynamic they see happening around them.

Meet in these pages also the first man who discovered how to water-ski, and learn the strange but inspiring story of how it happened.

On the Waters of the World is a story of an industrial pioneer and the family he raised, the boat company he started, the faith he passed on. Because one man remained true to the Christian gospel he embraced as a young man, the world today is not quite the same.

2

Storm Boats Cross the Rhine

January 1945. Adolph Hitler had just overplayed his hand in the Battle of the Bulge. In a massive counterattack against Allied forces, staged just before Christmas, his armies had inflicted major damage. But he had also suffered heavy losses—losses he could not afford. The Third Reich had begun to crumble.

General Dwight D. Eisenhower and his forces advanced rapidly, pushing steadily through France, Belgium, and across the borders into Germany. It was an all-out drive toward Berlin, but first they had to cross the Rhine. Since the time of Napoleon, this swift, muddy river had held Germany's enemies at bay.

Now the very success of the Allied drive posed his greatest problem. Because Eisenhower was weeks ahead of schedule, his armies were approaching the banks of the Rhine River without enough boats to make a safe crossing.

The general pondered his strategy. He knew he would face a crucial loss of time and troops unless he could cross the river quickly. He earmarked March 10 as the best date to cross the river.

Cabling an SOS to Washington, Eisenhower asked for a March delivery of 569 storm boats to the Rhine River. These compact seventeen-foot vessels with their spoon-shaped bows were tailor-made for such maneuvers. The highly expendable boats could skid up onto beaches at full throttle.

Eisenhower's suppliers could not delay. It was now early February, and strategic Allied gains could be lost unless they pressed their advantage. U.S. Army engineers quickly responded to the emergency. They began contacting boatbuilders across the country. High on their list was Correct Craft in Pine Castle, Florida, near Orlando.

The boat company had shut down that February 9 in honor of a friend's funeral being held in a nearby church. Walter C. Meloon, company founder (hereafter referred to as W.C. to avoid confusion with sons and grandsons), left for the service with his three sons, Walt, Ralph, and Harold. When they returned to the plant, the watchman handed W.C. a message.

Army engineers had been trying to reach him all afternoon, calling from a district office in Jacksonville, a division office in Atlanta, and the chief's office in Washington, D.C.

When W.C. returned the call, the chief engineer explained Eisenhower's situation. He asked, "How many storm boats can you build by February 28, with a triple-A preference rating and all the cooperation possible from the U.S. engineers?"

W.C. promised to reply after he held a family conference. What he really wanted was time to pray.

The firm's normal February schedule called for building 48 boats. How many could they trust the Lord for in this national emergency? How big was their faith? They finally committed the company to 300 storm boats—an impossible task, friends assured them. Yet they had confidence in God's ability to do the impossible as they did their part.

W.C. knew the firm couldn't do it without help from the Lord. The next day the plant geared up for the increased production. The Meloon family and their employees worked until midnight building jigs—open frames for holding work and guiding machine tools to the work. They made preliminary plans to start production. After stopping to rest on Sunday, they resumed work at 1:00 A.M. Monday. That day they increased their crew from 60 employees to 320.

Problems multiplied with scarcity of material, uncertain transportation, new and inexperienced help, and shortage of time. Army engineers sent help as they had promised: a plant engineer, a staff of inspectors, auditors, material, and labor expediters.

Still, only fifteen days remained to complete 300.

Trucks and airplanes scoured the United States in search of material to keep production going. Plywood was flown from the Pacific Northwest. Many times the material arrived as supplies gave out. It was winter. Some truck drivers crawled over mountainous roads when storms raged so fiercely that no other vehicles had ventured out. God carried them through without a single accident. It was an answer to prayer.

Government expediters offered many good suggestions. One of them, however, called for a seven-day workweek in view of the urgency involved. The Meloons responded with a polite but firm no.

"We intend to do the job to the glory of God," W.C. said. "It's not His plan to work seven days a week."

The government expediter argued that the company needed the three extra days to accomplish the task. The Meloons stood their ground, quoting Scripture: "Remember the sabbath day, to keep it holy" (Exodus 20:8, KJV*). "Them that honour me I will honour" (1 Samuel 2:30, KJV).

"If you insist," W.C. said, "you can have the contract back. This job is impossible for man to do alone."

The Meloons did not give in, even though they knew a possible legal battle with the government might wipe them out. Finally relenting, the engineers gave them per-

*King James Version.

mission to work only six days a week on the emergency job.

Similar conflicts arose at their other plant in Titus-ville. There the Meloons built boats for the navy, including plane-rearming boats, navy whaleboats, and plane personnel boats. Government policy restricted the awarding of contracts to builders from more than one branch of the service at a time. Providentially, the Meloons believe, contracts came from the army and navy on the same day and remained in effect with government approval.

A navy inspector told the firm it could not take time out for weekly chapel services. The boatbuilders again responded firmly.

"If we can't serve the Lord and the U.S. Navy at the same time, we just won't serve the navy."

The navy commander in Jacksonville finally realized the unyielding stand of the family and overruled his subordinate.

"You won't have any further problem with the inspector on this," he assured them.

On Monday, February 12, the company built one storm boat. What seemed like an agonizingly slow process began to improve. They built three boats on Tuesday and seven on Wednesday. Some of their own employees shook their heads in disbelief when the family called a halt for the midweek chapel service in the plant. With three of the fifteen days gone, only eleven boats had been built.

That night the entire family met together for prayer. They prayed more desperately than ever before, asking God to show them how to complete the job.

Walt, the oldest son, awakened the next morning with an idea that would speed production. A new machine and a change on the jig was the answer. He made the change and located a man who believed he could build the new machine. He needed the rest of the week to complete the work. Meanwhile, production accelerated with the change on the jig.

On Thursday, February 15, less than two weeks from their deadline, the workers built 13. On Friday they built 17. On Saturday, 21. Still, with six of the fifteen days gone, only 62 of the 300 boats had been built.

The work crew rested again on Sunday, then resumed production early Monday morning, February 19. Refreshed by the day of rest and with the new machine in action, they rapidly moved ahead.

What followed, journalist Jim Harmon wrote years later in *Powerboat* magazine,"was comparable to cramming two hours of music onto a 30-minute cassette."[1]

On Wednesday, February 21, an army officer flew down from Atlanta and marveled at the boats stacked all over the plant. Even the highway in front of the plant had been blocked off, with village, county, and state approval, to accommodate the overflow. A photo of that memorable scene—a street congested with boats—would appear late that same year in *National Geographic.*

The plant hummed with activity. By now the 320 men and women workers were building up to forty-two boats a day.

A local minister presided at the midweek chapel service. He invited the colonel to say a few words to the employees. Standing atop a cutting bench in the middle of the blocked-off Florida highway, the officer looked down into the faces of the workers.

"Men and women," he said, "you have done a remarkable job, and I want to compliment you. I have just visited three other plants in the north where they are working on this same job, and all of them together are not doing what you are doing."

1. Jim Harmon, "The Meloons: Three Parts Know-How, Three Parts Faith, *Powerboat*, August 1982.

Encouraged by the remarks and a conviction that God was working, the Meloons and their coworkers returned to their task with new zeal.

At noon on Saturday, February 24, a jubilant crew of boatbuilders stood on the sidetrack and saw an express train haul away the 306th boat. The army engineer in charge of the special project said, "There goes our quota four days ahead of schedule. Someone other than man did this job. If it had rained only one day, we couldn't have accomplished it."

A day earlier, the plant had received a special request from the chief of engineers.

Would they build another 100 boats?

The other three contractors, he said, had fallen short of their quota. The Meloons, their accelerated operation now in full swing, delivered 400 boats ahead of time! They were sent to New York in fruit trucks, the best ground transportation available at the time, and then were flown to Europe.

The boats were to be expendable—no recycling. One trip across, each packed with a dozen soldiers, would be their mission.

Plant workers prayed for the success of the Rhine crossing with extra fervor.

"When the storm boats produced by the other builders arrived at the Rhine," Walt says, "they couldn't use them. The specs were wrong, and the engines wouldn't fit. Ours were the only ones built right."

The Allies got an incredible break on the Rhine crossing when the Nazis failed to blow up a railroad bridge at Remagen before the Allies arrived. Hitler was furious. Two days later he executed the three men whom he held responsible for what may have been the greatest blunder of the war. Military experts, said *National Geographic,* "estimated that at least 15,000 American lives were saved by the miracle of Remagen."[2]

But the Meloons had also seen a miracle in their own boat plant.

On March 2, the same labor expediter who had urged Correct Craft to work seven days a week, returned to the plant.

He stood in front of the shop, tears glistening on his cheeks. "You folks certainly have faith in the Lord," he said. "I want to congratulate you." He shook hands with W.C. and his three sons.

On May 23, 1945, the United States government, in a special ceremony at the plant, awarded the firm the army and navy "E" award. In Washington, D.C., the government listed the boatbuilding achievement on their records as "the miracle production."

Visitors from all parts of the United States for many weeks thereafter came to see the place where a company could build 400 boats in fifteen days, without infringing on the Lord's Day.

The Meloon family attributed all honor to the God who had led and strengthened them. "To us," they said, "it was simply an indication that the Lord honors the obedience of His children."

2. "Winning the War in Supply," *National Geographic* (December 1945): 734.

3

The Man Who Invented Waterskiing

When Correct Craft delivered its storm boats for the Rhine, visitors came from around the country to tour the scene of a boatbuilding miracle. The firm was assured of at least a small role in military history. The U.S. government soon granted more contracts.

Yet the very assault boats that had earned fame would also help close down the war and military sales. The firm may have had little future without the recreational market.

Especially if man had not tried to ski on water.

As far back as 1927, the Meloons had established ties with Florida's famous Cypress Gardens, by supplying boats to its founder, Dick Pope. Together they popularized the sport of waterskiing.

The story of how waterskiing began is as fascinating and inspiring as the Meloons' own story. The account below, prepared in 1977 by Gregor Ziemer for the *Orlando Tribune* (forerunner of today's *Correct Craft Tribune* magazine), tells it well.

The majority of this chapter is reprinted from Gregor Ziemer, "Water Skiing's Inventor Recalls Debut on Minnesota Lake in 1922," *Orlando Tribune*, Spring-Summer 1977. On August 28, 1977, Ralph Samuelson went home to be with his Savior.

Not many sports can pinpoint the exact time of their beginning.

Thanks to Ralph Samuelson, water skiing can.

More than 50 million water skiers (12 million of them in the U.S.A.), ranging from 4 to 80, know the exact time when a young man became the first to slide along on top of water. It happened at 4:11 P.M., Sunday, July 2, 1922, on Lake Pepin, a bulge of the Mississippi, 60 miles below the Twin Cities.

But for 40 years after that not even the American Water Ski Association knew for certain where the fast-growing sport had originated. Seattle claimed it happened there; so did Cypress Gardens, Florida; even the French Riviera. But not Lake City.

Why the uncertainty?

Because Ralph Samuelson let people forget what he had done. He never patented his skis.

At the time he was a sort of happy-go-lucky heathen, a tall, rangy Swede who hadn't been in church since he was nine, when his best friend, Vernie Johnson, was tossed out of the sanctuary after blow-gunning the Swedish preacher with a pea.

Sammy just grew up, never went to Sunday school, never read the Bible. He was too busy helping to support a family of five kids and an alcoholic father. He worked in the local nursery, pulling weeds, became a fisherman, and a clammer, even owned his own boat at one time. He knew and loved Lake Pepin.

But always, since he was 10, he was possessed by one idea. "Every winter my brothers and I ski on snow; why can't we ski on water in the summer?"

And every summer he tried it with different devices, snow skis, barrel staves, while being towed by Brother Ben's stinking clamming boat. But when the towline tightened, down went Sammy, to join the clams.

One summer day in 1922, Ralph left the clamming boat with its long iron bar from which dangled clamming hooks, and wandered down to the local Botsford Lumber yard, a few blocks from his modest frame home on Washington Street, and bought two planks, each 8 feet long and 9 inches wide, for $2 (on credit).

He stuck the tips into his carpet-weaving mother's copper wash kettle, boiled them for three hours, secured them in a vise, kept them under stress for two days until they were permanently curved. He nailed a piece of rubber matting to each, and a leather strap, marked them "R" and "L," for he considered it important to have the [correct] ski on the proper foot. Then, holding on to an old clothesline, with a metal ring wound with tape, out they went again to deep water.

But again and again, down went Sammy. . . .

By now it was Sunday . . . and most people went to church. Not Sammy. He was out on the lake all morning.

And then it happened.

"I didn't deserve it, but God had plans for me, so at 4:11 P.M. a voice told me to keep the tips of my monstrous skis *out* of the water when I started. And there I was. Skimming on top of the waves like a water bug. Not that anybody cared," says Ralph. "But it was a great satisfaction to me. I had finally proved to my friends that I was not a complete fool.

"But I didn't have the faintest idea what I had started."

It's as Tom Hardman, editor and publisher of the official *Water Skier* says, "If we had a way of foreordaining these things, we couldn't have picked a finer Father of Water Skiing than Ralph Samuelson. He has been an amazing asset to the sport ever since he discovered it on Lake Pepin in Minnesota, largely because of his modesty and his genuine wonderment of what he started quite innocently back in 1922."

That wonderment has never left Ralph.

"I was still completely unaware that by becoming the world's first water-skier God was giving me a tool, which I would eventually use in his service. . . ."

Ralph, who turned 19 the day after his big success, continued to improve his technique, gave skiing demonstrations on the lake, but never earned a penny with his new skill. All entrance fees collected at the Sunday water carnivals were used by the Chamber of Commerce to buy land for a modern marina.

The next summer Ralph became the world's first water-ski jumper, off a tilted diving platform. At first he nearly had his arm yanked out, and his rump tattooed with splinters, until he greased the boards with lard from Huettle's meat market.

In 1925 Samuelson added another first, when he skied 80 miles per hour behind Walter Bullock's reconstructed World War I Flying Boat.

Then . . . Ralph and his gigantic skis motored to Detroit to visit a cousin, performed on the dirty Detroit River, then drove south to Florida, where Ralph's father had invested in land. He ·gave exhibitions on Lake Worth, near Lantana, and on the ocean off Palm Beach.

"I was riding high," says Ralph. "I loved the adulation of the crowds. I really was a fool then. But not yet God's fool."

One day while helping to build a new dock, Ralph was holding up a section of wooden platform so a trench could be dug underneath. Supporting props gave way, a friend panicked, and single-handedly Ralph held up the boards long enough for a fellow-worker to scramble to safety.

He saved the man's life, but broke his back—a compression fracture. He was an invalid. Waterskiing was ended, forever.

Ralph was bitter. Why did God, if there was a God, let this happen to him?

Back in Lake City, the two skis went up into the rafters of an old fish house. Ralph mended a little, took a job as skipper of a rich man's yacht, married an Irish girl, moved to a small farm, decided to try raising turkeys.

And much to the surprise of his friends, he succeeded —year after year—until he was actually the biggest turkey farmer in the state, with the most modern equipment —brooders, feeders, hatcheries, air-conditioned trucks.

Ralph became rich—owned Lincoln Continentals, a fleet of racing boats, an airplane, spent vacations in Canada hunting moose.

"Then God really fixed me," says Ralph. "He took me down 20 pegs. It began when I learned that my wife was unfaithful to me—had been for 10 years. Everybody knew it but me."

The blow to Ralph's ego, his pride, almost was fatal. He contemplated suicide.

"Then one night, out under His stars, while I was shouting to Him to help me or end my life, God spoke to me, laid His hand on me, saved me. I became His," Ralph said. How it happened he doesn't know. Why it happened Ralph does know.

"He wanted me to work for Him. But, sadly enough, I still wasn't ready. Oh, I had changed, had given up smoking, drinking, cursing. I found a beautiful new wife, Hazel Thorpe, whom God let me discover Christmas morning in church, where I saw her at a distance, and heard Him say, 'There is your real wife.' "

Yes, Ralph was going to church now, he and Hazel were married in a church. (Doctors had told her she could never have children. Ralph says he prayed for children. He is now the father of [two daughters and one son].

Success stayed with Ralph. Business got better and better, until he owned a $500,000 spread—farms, hatcheries, a beautiful dream house.

Then it happened again. "This time God was really tired of my pride, I guess," says Ralph. "He made me feel as Job must have felt—at his worst."

In three successive years plague hit Ralph's beautiful flocks of bronze turkeys, in spite of what the best experts in the country could do: cholera, erysipelas, paratyphoid.

Ralph had to declare bankruptcy.

The wealthy, influential tycoon was suddenly a nobody.

"The only thing that kept me going was my faith. I felt, somehow, that eventually God was going to use me, although I didn't know how. Time after time I nearly despaired," says Ralph. "I wanted to work for Him, but I was nothing—dirt. It seems in our country, nowadays, people don't want to listen to nobodies, certainly not to a busted, retired turkey farmer. 'What has God done for you? Nothing,' my friends told me. They said the faith I was yapping about was foolish. Once more I was a fool."

The skis?

"God works in mysterious ways," recalls Ralph. "He finally used those same old skis in a way I never would have suspected."

This is what happened:

When Ralph was still owner of his big farm, and the skis were up in the big barn's rafters, a young man who had seen Ralph do his first stunt on water skis had become the harbor master of Lake City, Ben Simons.

The town still had annual water carnivals. Ben wanted an eye-catching display for the biggest window in town, that of Collins' Drug Store. He remembered those big old skis. Where were they? Where was Ralph Samuelson?

After a search Ben found him counting turkeys. Together they resurrected the skis, Ben cleaned them, put then on display with a homemade sign, "World's First Water Skis."

"I never knew one small town could have so many skeptics," Ben said. Nobody believed they were the world's first. So after the carnival I tucked them away in the attic of a store we owned. There they lay until 1963 when the city built itself a new bathhouse, and I needed some wall decorations. Instead of hanging up bathing beauties, I took another chance on the old skis, and nailed them up, with the same old sign."

"That summer God took another step," says Ralph, "and I didn't know it until later."

A young sportswriter of the St. Paul *Pioneer-Press,* Margaret Crimmins, was spending a vacation at Lake City, visited the bathhouse, saw the old skis, got all excited, actually tried them out, wrote a feature about them, which appeared in the next Sunday's edition. "Your old skis are great. Where are you, Mr. Samuelson?"

Ralph saw it, and suddenly God's purpose was becoming clear. He was to be anonymous no longer. He would be known again. Then perhaps people would listen to him while he witnessed for Christ.

And so it came to pass.

First Ralph, Margaret, and Ben made a pilgrimage to the St. Paul Historical Society, dug up old copies of now defunct 1922 newspapers to prove, with pictures, that Ralph had actually water-skied in 1922. They wrote to the American Water Ski Association, Winter Haven, Florida, with corroborating evidence, and statements by eye-witnesses.

It upset the Association—and a few million water-skiers!

But eventually Ralph's challenge won. The other claimants, including the French Riviera, had to admit Ralph had done it first. He was officially proclaimed Father of Water Skiing.

In 1972, when Lake City celebrated its centennial, and simultaneously the 50th anniversary of water skiing,

Ralph gained more nation-wide, world-wide publicity on radio, television, and in the press. At the dedication of an Historical Society plaque by the shore of Lake Pepin, he and his famous skis were photographed hundreds of times.

A few years later, September 1976, Lake City unveiled another monument in his honor, a huge stylized wave, near the actual cove where Ralph first came up out of the water like an apparition.

Again in his speech Ralph gave all credit to God: "Without Him I would be nothing. He has brought me out of anonymity to let me spread the message—that He is great."

In the newly dedicated Water Ski Hall of Fame, near Disney World in Florida, Exhibit No. 1 is the old skis. Once bought for $2, they are now priceless relics. . . .

And people will still remember Ralph Samuelson in 2076, because in the time capsule that will be opened at Valley Forge at our Tricentennial, is a bronze replica of his first skis.

4
From Cypress Gardens to Sea World

Ralph Samuelson may have been the first man to water-ski, but it was Dick Pope, founder of Florida's Cypress Gardens, who teamed up with the Meloons and their recreational boats to popularize the sport.

At his modest lake resort in Winter Haven, near Orlando, Dick Pope introduced waterskiing to the local public as early as 1930. It was simply a novelty then, not an organized sport. In those days Cypress Gardens did not exist, although the theme park emerged later on the same general site.

Ralph Meloon still recalls those days.

"Dad started his boat business near Orlando in 1925. Two years later he started towing gliders behind his boats. We used freeboards, aquaplanes, water skis—all kinds of contraptions to attract crowds to the waterfront where we could take people for boat rides—twenty-five cents for adults and ten cents for children," he says.

"Dad also built speedboats and raced them. Usually he won. We'd often stage shows on Lake Ivanhoe, now Orlando's prime site for water-ski tournaments."

But the boats needed public exposure in order to sell. The Meloons would offer rides to the public and look for new promotional twists, like their water toboggan powered by a large outboard motor.

"We'd stand people on it and take them for a cruise. One day we decided to put a little Austin car on it. That idea almost backfired. When the toboggan came to an abrupt stop, the center weight of the car automatically moved forward enough that the toboggan went up on its nose and dumped the Austin into the middle of the lake. We had to fish it out of the lake bottom as the crowd looked on with glee.

"It turned out to be the best part of the show, except that we had borrowed the Austin from a local car agency. The owner thought the incident less than funny. Until it later brought him all kinds of good publicity.

"Our family put on water-ski shows all across the deep South—through Tennessee and the Carolinas—and up the East Coast. Dick Pope, nicknamed 'Mr. Florida,' the greatest promoter I've ever known, saw the popularity of our shows and conceived the idea of Cypress Gardens —which he developed from an estate he later acquired from John Snivley.

"Dick used to hire me," says Ralph, "to drive him and prospective investors from Winter Haven's Lake Howard through back waterways to Lake Louise, the current heart of Cypress Gardens. I was only a teenager, and I didn't realize at the time the significance of these excursions."

When Cypress Gardens became reality, the boats of the Florida Variety Boat Company—later Correct Craft —garnished the waters of Lake Louise. Pope bought his first boat from the Meloons for fifty dollars. For nearly a half century he used almost no other boats, despite the fact that Cypress Gardens and the Meloons never had a written agreement between them—so trusting was the relationship.

During World War II the fleet of assault boats that the Meloons built to attack Hitler's armies catapulted the company name among government contractors and gave the firm further business. But as military construction wound down, government contracts faded. To keep the business afloat, the Meloons turned once again to entertainment and recreation.

Their boats continued to gain prominence in this arena. At Cypress Gardens Jordan's King Hussein I waterskied for the first time behind a twenty-foot Correct Craft Tournament Skier. He liked the boat so well he later bought four Correct Craft boats for his own use.

Cypress Gardens may have first introduced waterskiing to the world in the 1930s, but its popularity as a sport grew gradually. While Dick Pope drew bigger crowds to his Florida theme park over the decades, Correct Craft was perfecting its speedboats. In 1960 it introduced what would become the "limousine" of the waterski tow boats: the Ski Nautique. Waterskiing grew as a professional sport, and today, among the world's professionals, the Ski Nautique has earned global acclaim.

In 1985 Cypress Gardens celebrated fifty years of success with an aquacade that boasted one of the largest collections of water sports champions in the world. Millions each year come to see Cypress Gardens' swimming, diving, and skiing spectaculars. Acres of blooming flowers continue to mark the origin of the gardens etched out of the swamps by Dick and Julie Pope more than fifty years ago, which eventually developed into one of the most photographed and recognized areas in the world.

Other offerings include a unique antebellum village, a natural wildlife section, the largest model railroad exhibit in Florida, and a series of shows involving alligators, magic, and performing birds. Visitors also can ride on the Island in the Sky, rotating 153 feet above the ground for a spectacular view of the surrounding area.

In 1985, Harcourt Brace Jovanovich, internationally known book publishers, purchased Cypress Gardens, ending fifty years of independent ownership. Dick Pope, its founder, has been installed into the Water Ski Hall of Fame.

Although Cypress Gardens' shows currently do not spotlight Correct Craft, they are used at Sea World in Orlando, Cleveland, and San Antonio, Texas. Two million visitors a year attend these two attractions.

The themes of these Correct Craft-sponsored shows change each year. At the Sea World 1985 show in Orlando, crowds laughed, gasped, and applauded as the precision skiers, pulled by Correct Craft Ski Nautiques, performed their water version of the "Hatfields and Mc-Coys," complete with floating houseboats, tin lizzies, gunshot explosions, and diving revenuers. The next year the theme turned to "Beach Blanket Ski Party," with colorful sets and costumes in a tongue-in-cheek look at beach parties, hamburger hangouts, surfing, and hot-rodding.

If all of this seems to project the carefree life of California surfing as the ultimate satisfaction, there is another side to what is really happening behind the scenes at Sea World. While still fun-loving at heart, growing numbers of these young performers are discovering that real joy has its roots in the spiritual side of life. A key catalyst in the Christian movement there is Andy Hansen, Sea World's Ski Show director, who has a story of his own to tell.

"Early in my professional skiing days I demanded all the attention I could bring to myself through being the best skier, organizing the best parties, being the arm wrestling champion, drinking the most beer, having the nicest stereo system, and dating the prettiest, most popular girls."

Then came the setbacks.

The first two were serious automobile accidents, one of which left him with a broken back. Then Hansen nearly drowned when he was trapped under the water with no air and no apparent escape. Later, he fell nearly three hundred feet when his delta wing kite collapsed.

After four close calls with death, "God really started to get my attention," Hansen says. "One night one of the girls at the ski show invited me to a Bible study at her home. Her father led the study. People asked questions. I was amazed to hear some of the truths from the Bible. The girl's father described what it meant to have a personal relationship with Jesus Christ. We were all given a free will to accept or reject Christ, he explained. It was God's grace that He gave us the gift of His son, and through belief in Him we could be saved. There was nothing we could do on our own but to open our hearts and let Christ come in."[1]

In time Hansen did just that.

It was also at Sea World that Bill Peterson made the same discovery. Today he and his wife run a well-known ski school in Windermer, Florida. There, scores of young people and others who train under his expertise also hear the Christian message.

Spinoff sports such as boat surfing have grown out of waterskiing. In 1964, skiers at Florida's Cypress Gardens started boat surfing, which replaces water skis with a surfboard and the action of ocean waves with boat power. Once up to speed, the skier can drop the towrope and use his arms to help balance himself as he rides the wake, until he finally wipes out. Surfers no longer have to seek out the ocean to enjoy surfing, for now any lake, river, or bay will do. Some call it "inland surfing" or "instant ocean."

Whatever the variation, the boat plays a key role. And Correct Craft has earned a reputation for the finest craftsmanship. But it didn't happen overnight. The story of the firm cannot be properly told apart from the story of the Meloons themselves and the moral and spiritual values that motivate the family members even today.

1. *Correct Craft Tribune*, Summer 1985.

5

Yankee Boatbuilder

In the small village of Ossipee, New Hampshire, the Meloon and Hamm families became close friends. They belonged to the same church, and the children attended the same school. As they reached their teens, two of them—W. C. Meloon and Marion Adiena Hamm—began to show interest in each other.

W.C. dropped out of high school after two years to work in a little print shop that advertised Hamm's Balm-Elixir Company, which made a patent medicine liniment—a strong formula for horses, a weaker one for people. W.C. often walked home with Mr. Hamm and stayed for supper. One evening, while helping Marion with the dishes, he asked her to marry him.

Marion said she couldn't unless he became a Christian. She had accepted Christ as her Savior a couple of years earlier and knew that Christians should not be "unequally yoked together with unbelievers" (2 Corinthians 6:14, KJV).

"I have become a Christian," W.C. assured her, "and I'll make a public profession as soon as I can." Their church was closed at the time for lack of a pastor.

The couple married a short time later. They migrated to Buffalo, New York, in 1914. W.C. worked first with the Hooker Chemical Company in Niagara Falls and later in St. Catherines, Ontario, helping with the construction of a high-level bridge. He then worked with his older brother, Nat, who operated the Buffalo Bronze Die Casting

Corporation. The company manufactured the big gear for the Ford Model T one-ton truck before the Detroit motor firm began to make its own gears.

Later, Nat Jr. and his brother Hank followed in their father's footsteps and operated the Meloon Bronze Foundry in Syracuse, New York. (To this day this firm manufactures struts, rudders, and water gear for Correct Craft boats.)

Early in his marriage, W.C. settled his spiritual vow. When evangelist Lee Aldrich came to Buffalo for a week of meetings, W.C. went forward to make a public commitment. He was baptized, joined the Baptist church, and began to take his Christianity seriously.

A week after his public profession, he accidently hammered his thumb and swore. Promptly overwhelmed with guilt and shame, he asked God's forgiveness. Years later, in intense pain after he caught his hand in an air-compressor V-belt and broke a finger, he simply said, "I believe I broke a finger."

W.C. loved to tinker with all kinds of machinery. He spent much spare time building a boat powered by a Ford Model T engine driving an old airplane propeller. That hobby set in motion the business that would later catapult his name into the highest ranks of the recreational boating industry.

In the early years of their marriage W.C. and Marion moved frequently, trying various jobs, anxious to learn what the Lord had in mind for them. From Buffalo the two moved back to Ossipee, where W.C. went into the garage business.

They acquired two garages. Both burned down. One fire started from an electric motor that ignited some gasoline. The other erupted from live ashes dumped in back of a stable connected to the garage. W.C. and Marion lost materials that required twenty years to repay. They had no insurance to cover the loss.

By now they had two sons: Walter O., born in 1915 at Niagara Falls, and Ralph C., born in 1917 in Ossipee. Harold E. followed in 1920 in Providence, Rhode Island. But in spite of her busyness as a mother, Marion still found time to keep the books for the business. She had completed a brief business course and had good business sense. As the children grew old enough to help out at home, she put in many long days at the office without pay. Not until World War II did she agree to accept a modest salary.

W.C. was a wonderful father. With all three sons on his knees he would tell them bedtime stories about Buffalo Bill and Wild Bill Hickok, always stopping at the height of suspense with a promise to continue the next night.

W.C. later sold Ford and Dodge cars before pioneering a different kind of business. Buying a small piece of property on nearby Duncan Lake, New Hampshire, they built the first tourist cabins the region had ever known. They sold the property in 1925 to move to Florida after persistent urging by two of W.C.'s sisters.

W.C. had already observed the scarcity of boats in Florida, despite its many lakes. It seemed natural for him to establish the Florida Variety Boat Company, with himself as president. Even the name of the firm allowed plenty of room for experimenting—just what W.C. wanted.

The Yankee invader built his first plant in a central Florida garden spot called Pine Castle, so named by a Florida poet and promoter, William Wallace Harney, who built a castle in the pines in 1870. In these pleasant surroundings W.C. struggled with the early growing pains of his boatbuilding firm. His first partner stayed with him just a year, saw no future in the business, and sold his interest. The next partner lasted five years and also sold out.

Florida Variety Boat Company made no great ripples in the industry during those early years. In 1930 it became known as the Pine Castle Boat and Construction Company. Eight years later a radio commercial extolling the virtues of "the correct heel for your shoe" gave W.C. the idea for a new company name. *Great,* he thought, *why not "the correct craft for you"?* The rest is history. Soon his company began calling its products Correct Craft. The firm was incorporated in 1947.

During the early thirties, depression stalked the nation, and began to take its toll on the boating industry. Three bank failures cost the Meloons all they had. After the second failure, the company sold a dozen boats to officials at Lake Placid, Florida, a tourist attraction one hundred miles south of Orlando. The buyers would pay only a token down payment. After repeated attempts to get the money owed them, the Meloons drove to Lake Placid, collected the three hundred dollars due, and placed it in a bank on Saturday, along with other small checks they had received. The bank closed on Monday.

Marion Meloon promptly called all the check writers and asked them to stop payment. The bank had to return the original checks, and their writers wrote new ones. Marion's quick thinking salvaged something from a disaster.

The boat company paid its employees on Saturdays. W.C. often scurried around to sell a rowboat or runabout, sometimes below cost, to get a few dollars to divide up on payday. Once he took his wife's last ten dollars to pay five workers so that they could buy groceries. W.C. increased production during one period by nailing a one-dollar bill to the wall for each man in the plant.

"When you finish the boat you're working on," he told them, "you can claim your one-dollar bill."

6
Silver Dollars

When World War II triggered a sudden upsurge in boatbuilding, W.C. and his sons began to seek a logical site for a second plant. They found it at Titusville, fifty miles east of Pine Castle on the Atlantic Coast near what is now Cape Kennedy.

Convinced that building a Correct Craft plant in the town would enhance its economy, Titusville officials gave property to the Meloons on a sixty-year lease.

Neither Titusville nor the Meloons, however, had counted on the opposition of World War II veterans. The property had been dedicated as a park, and the veterans insisted it would take an act of the legislature to sell it.

W.C.'s son Walt appeared at a special city council hearing called to reconsider the gift and discuss what a potential multimillion-dollar contract could do for the city.

His appearance, however, only seemed to stir up the opposition. Some wanted to break the lease and evict the Meloons from the city. The government stood by with a number of contracts, one for nineteen-foot boats needed for the Korean War. Before those contracts could be granted, however, Correct Craft needed to increase its net worth so it could obtain a bond issue to cover the contracts—for a total of 400 boats.

Opponents of the plan sought support up and down the streets. Feelings became so negative that Walt's wife, Ann, feared to go to the grocery store. Council members began to reconsider their gift of property to the boat-builders. The firm's cause seemed almost hopeless.

Then Walt encountered a friend, Dewey Fisk, who suggested a maneuver he had seen work successfully in a similar situation.

"I know a fellow who paid his entire payroll one time in silver dollars," Fisk said. "That way he knew where the money was being spent. If you will do the same, the business people in this city will know where their money is coming from."

Walt had no other ideas.

"The silver dollars will have to come from the Federal Reserve Bank in Atlanta," he was told.

A few days later, bank officials delivered a wheel-barrow full of silver dollars to Correct Craft. They placed the money in bags with employees' names on them.

About thirty minutes after distributing the payroll, the manager of the local A. & P. grocery called the plant.

"Walt, don't pull that trick again," he pleaded. "I can't close my cash drawer!"

Other stores had similar problems. Headlines the next morning read: "Correct Craft Pays Payroll in Silver Dollars; Chokes Cash Registers."

The point was made. A week later, the Meloons offered the city one dollar for the property. City council members called a special meeting to act on the offer.

"I move that we keep Correct Craft and let them have the property so they can get this contract," a councilman began. One of his colleagues seconded the motion, and the council passed it unanimously without debate.

In the days that followed, bankers from several towns and cities came to Titusville and offered loans to Correct Craft so it could build the planned factory.

Ray Carroll, president of the First National Bank of Kissimmee, in cooperation with twelve other banks, arranged to lend W.C. half a million dollars. But a few days later, Carroll came to the boat executive in deep distress.

"Mr. Meloon," he said, "I'm in terrible shape. The bank examiner has just come and declared the loan illegal. He is going to close all our banks. We would have to have mortgages on property to cover all this."

At that strategic moment, a representative of the city of Titusville delivered the property deed.

"Ray," W.C. asked, "would this be enough to get the examiners off our backs?"

It proved to be the lifesaving move. The examiners were satisfied. The First National Bank of Kissimmee continued to loan money to Correct Craft for years.

Meanwhile, an editorial in the Titusville newspaper helped to bolster the Correct Craft relationship with the city. "Estimating four to a family," the editorial read, "the total number of people living off the Correct Craft payroll is 1,040, which is about a third or fourth of our population. This does not take into consideration the indirect benefits of a plant like that in a community."

Walt became general manager of the Titusville plant, which soon had three hundred employees on its rolls. Correct Craft remained in the East Coast city from 1942 to 1955. The Titusville plant was sold in 1960 and was later leveled to the ground. It had served its purpose in the booming post-war years, although the plant may never have existed had it not been for the well-timed delivery of a property deed—and a wheelbarrow full of silver dollars.

7

One Part Know-How;
One Part Faith

The year was 1931, the heart of the depression. Somehow the Meloon family kept their boat business going, however precariously. The sons did their best to help out. Ralph, at age twelve, began taking company boats to nearby lakes to bring in a little money for groceries and to keep the struggling firm afloat.

Walt and two of his cousins, Fred and Bud Jones, helped in the beginning. Later his Uncle Cal and one of the firm's employees joined Ralph, and they began to make longer trips.

The crew traveled from town to town with boats on top of the car or pulled behind, going from one lake to another in search of business. They announced the boat rides by loudspeaker in the town square.

"Only ten and twenty-five cents!" they shouted.

Then they would drive to a nearby lake, launch a boat, and wait for customers.

W.C. paid the men three dollars a week. They traveled six to eight weeks at a time, and had hamburger—their only meat—usually once during that period. Cal would buy wormy grits and float the worms off. That provided most of their diet. At night they slept on garage floors, usually managing to cover up with sheets. They often saw wharf rats a foot long.

Later, the family put two cars on the road and began to use larger boats, thus attracting larger crowds.

The New England Puritan work ethic, part of the Meloon heritage, remained strong in the family, but W.C. knew by now that life also had its spiritual side. The Reverend O. G. Hall, pastor of the Pine Castle Baptist Church, and W.C. became close friends. They spent hours talking about spiritual matters and church business.

Under the pastor's wise counsel, W.C. became convinced the Lord would help him pay his bills if he worked only six days a week instead of seven. He set the company policy to prohibit Sunday work. Soon he found himself able to pay not only his own bills but also pastor Hall's college debt.

Prayer became a natural part of W.C.'s life-style, and he was not ashamed of it among his colleagues. That was especially evident in 1951 when union men tried to organize the Correct Craft plant in Titusville.

At the time, Max K. Aulick, later a public relations figure with Correct Craft, operated both the Southern Lighting Manufacturing Company and the Orlando Boat Company. His firms made gas tanks for Correct Craft boats and helped to manufacture some components for the first military aluminum bridge-erection boats, also built by the Meloons.

During the meetings with the union men, Aulick noticed that they suddenly discontinued their efforts to organize Correct Craft.

"Why did you drop Correct Craft?" he asked.

"Do you want to know the truth?" responded the union negotiator.

"Yes," Aulick said.

"Every time we went over there and started a meeting to discuss negotiations, W.C. Meloon insisted on praying before the discussion began. The union organizer got so tired of the praying he decided to forget the whole thing."

Anxious to see every loved one have faith in Jesus Christ, W.C. looked for ways to share a natural witness. When he took a trip to South Carolina to pick up some fiberglass materials, he invited a grandson, Ralph Jr. (now president of Pacific Coast Correct Craft), to accompany him. Then, carefully and tactfully, he spent much of the travel time discussing the young man's life-style. W.C. exercised a similarly strong spiritual influence over all his family.

A photographer for the *Orlando Sentinel-Star* newspaper, assigned to take pictures at the Titusville plant several times, would occasionally have lunch or dinner with W.C. "Your dad taught me to give thanks at the table," he told Harold one day.

That same dependence on divine aid carried over into every area of W.C.'s life. Anxious to share his faith with his employees as an extension of his Sunday worship, he conducted his first chapel service at the Titusville plant in 1943. Eight years later, Billy Graham attracted the largest chapel attendance ever at Correct Craft when one thousand visitors overflowed the plant. Many received Christ as Savior that day.

Later, Grady Wilson and four other Billy Graham team members—Cliff Barrows, Beverly Shea, Paul Mikelsen, and Tedd Smith—held a week of services at both plants. Sam Meanes, a seventy-six-year-old rancher-oilman-cowboy from West Texas, spent his entire honeymoon with his new bride at the Pine Castle plant services. Many decisions resulted from the dual meetings.

Pioneers in industrial evangelism, the Meloons have continued chapel services through the years, although now they are held four times a year instead of weekly. Employees are not required to attend, but many do.

One longtime employee credited W.C.'s consistent life, more than the chapel services, with making the deepest impression on him.

"He was as close to me as any man could ever be outside of my own dad," truck driver Slim Guntrie said. "I worked with him day in and day out. He never asked an employee to do anything that he wouldn't do himself. He always had time to say a cheery word to you no matter where you were. When he was intent on business, nothing else mattered—his clothes or his own well-being.

"One cold December day we were putting in a boat dock on a lake. He drove the car right down to the edge of the water, then walked out into the water in his good clothes, up to his waist, showing me where the dock should go.

"When he came out of the water he warned me, 'I've got to stay out of Mother's sight until my clothes dry or she'll kill me.' "

It was not uncommon to find W.C.'s shirts and ties scattered around the plant where he had removed them to perform some task.

On one occasion his wife phoned Correct Craft executive Norman Sewell to alert him.

"Will you watch out for some bankers who are coming to the plant today?" she asked. "We're anxious to make a good impression so we can get a loan. Be sure to see that Dad is properly dressed when they come."

When the bankers arrived, they began to ask questions about W.C.; Sewell thought it best to pave the way for whatever they might find. "If you see someone with his sleeves rolled up," he suggested, "that will probably be Mr. Meloon."

But what they did not expect to see was a grease-covered man lifting up a boat. Fortunately, what they saw impressed them. Not every firm had its president pitching in to do even the dirtiest work.

W.C. possessed a calmness and serenity that surprised and sometimes frustrated his friends. He refused to acknowledge anyone as his enemy. When a man with a real or imagined grievance avoided him on the sidewalk one day as they passed, W.C. walked briskly around the block. He confronted his "enemy" again and engaged him in friendly conversation. Competitors and creditors found it impossible to remain angry with him.

Even W.C.'s competitors considered him a top designer and promoter who was ahead of his time. They knew he did not hesitate to venture into new fields of boat design. He summed up his philosophy of work in a couplet: "If we are to give our employer his best, we must get our night's rest." When the clock struck 9:00 P.M. he would excuse himself and go to bed.

Until his death in 1974, W.C. spent time on his knees beside his bed each evening. When burdens troubled him during the night, he arose and prayed until the Lord satisfied him that everything was all right.

8

Government Inspectors

In 1955, W.C. retired from the firm he had founded, and his oldest son, Walter O. (called Walt), became company president.

Walt had learned the boat business from bow to stern. But not without first wandering off on his own like the prodigal son.

In his mid-teens Walt lost interest in school, so the family put him to work full time in the plant. At seventeen he left the company to join top rival Jack Dunn Chris-Craft, as a distributor, first in Old Forge, New York, then in Daytona, Florida. W.C. gave his approval. His mother dissented.

After two years with Jack Dunn Chris-Craft, Walt's wanderings took him to Palm Beach, Florida, where he worked for the Sea Phantom Company. Meanwhile, he "graduated" from the drugstore soda fountain to beer joints and picked up a tobacco pipe along the way.

Walt had been in Palm Beach about a year when he received a wire from his parents urging him to come home and take a job that was open.

Grasping the wire in one hand, Walt went out to the boatyard.

"See here," he said to his coworkers. "They finally have discovered they can't do without me at home."

With that attitude, plus a pipe in his mouth, Walt walked into his mother's kitchen a few days later. As he entered, she walked out. Walt's grandmother, also in the room, stood her ground.

"Walter," she began, "don't you ever do that again. You have broken your mother's heart."

Walt went back to work for the family firm, convinced by this time that other pastures were not so green after all. He matured, anchored himself spiritually, and in 1943 became a charter member of Orlando's Christian Businessmen's Committee (CBMC). He helped the Gideons in Bible distribution. In Titusville he served as a church deacon. When the town elected him president of its Chamber of Commerce, cocktail parties and dances were conspicuously absent.

In 1945, at a boat show in Philadelphia, Walt met Norman Sewell, a highly successful businessman and vice president of ten organizations. Sewell showed up at the show to see Correct Craft's first plywood boat. The two liked what they saw in each other and had a wonderful time talking about both the Lord and boats. In 1951, Sewell joined Correct Craft.

When Walt was named president, he promptly made Sewell his export manager. It was a good move. Sewell represented Correct Craft at international trade fairs with dignity, tact, and diplomacy. Export business climbed.

After World War II, the company moved into bigger boats—up to fifty-footers selling for $86,000. Then came a government contract for three thousand boats. The future looked bright.

Until the day when a government inspector dropped a bombshell.

That day the chief of a three-man inspection team sat across the table from Walt and Ralph as they sought to iron out details of the contract. The chief inspector eyed the papers suspiciously.

"Did you know," he said, "that you're one of only two companies in the whole Southeast who do not have someone on their payroll who carries an expense account to take care of the inspectors' expenses?" His smile seemed rather grim.

"No, I didn't," Walt said, feeling his way carefully. Walt knew the government took care of such expenses— and that the expense report scheme was a payoff through double reimbursement.

The inspector's sullen look made Correct Craft officials uneasy.

Two weeks later, when sixteen-foot fiberglass boats began coming down the production line, Ralph approached Walt with concern etched on his face. "Those government people are rejecting an awful lot of boats," he said.

"Well," Walt replied, "we don't want to deliver anything that isn't right."

"True," Ralph said, "but tiny blemishes are clearly allowable under terms of the contract."

When the high rate of rejections continued, Correct Craft tried an experiment. Selecting one of the rejected boats, they cleaned off the inspector's chalk marks and sent it back through the line on a later shift. This time it passed inspection.

The silent war continued. At times the Meloons thought, *Why not pay the man off? It really isn't much compared to what the company stands to lose.*

"It wasn't the money," Walt says today, "but something far deeper. At night I'd lie awake wrestling with the problem. Trying not to disturb my wife, Ann, I would slip out of bed, go to the living room, and kneel on the floor, my open Bible on a stool before me." (Ann always knew when Walt slipped out of bed to pray; she would pray, too.)

"I would talk with the Lord," Walt remembers, "and He would lead me through His Word. In the light of my living room lamp one night, these words seemed to glow: 'Trust in the Lord with all thine heart; and lean not unto thine own understanding. In all thy ways acknowledge him, and he shall direct thy paths' [Proverbs 3:5-6, KJV].

"That had to be our answer. To pay off the man would not be trusting the Lord but, rather, giving in to the devious ways of the world."

The family tried many avenues of financial relief. They found nothing but closed doors. Rejected boats piled up in the storage yard. Reading the Bible one night, Walt wondered if the Lord had forgotten them. He expressed his concern in prayer. An inner voice responded. *Have you forgotten the storm boats and what I did for you then?*

Perhaps he had lost sight too soon of the miracle production.

The family decided it would do what it could, short of dishonesty, to satisfy the government. By year's end the firm had delivered 2,200 boats. Six hundred rejects remained in the storage yard.

Then came the final blow.

A flatcar had just been loaded with forty "approved" boats. The chief inspector suddenly appeared just as the switch engine backed up to the flatcar. He turned to Walt.

"I don't like their looks," he said, pointing to the boats. "They've got to be unloaded and refinished."

That arbitrary decision, unfair as it was, made it impossible to continue. The contract already had cost the company one million dollars, and Correct Craft now owed half a million dollars to 228 creditors. Also, the bank had withdrawn all its commitments.

At a special meeting, the creditors heard the full story. Correct Craft promised to pay them as soon as possible and asked for suggestions.

One creditor recommended that the firm seek protection under chapter 11 of the Bankruptcy Act, which allows management to continue in the interest of creditors.

Others agreed to that implicit vote of confidence in the Meloon integrity, and in August 1958 that step was taken. But how could they build boats without money?

"I'll never forget that night when I walked into our silent plant," Walt recalls. "The floor that once hummed with busy workers was now deserted. I knew how Joseph must have felt as he was dragged down the long dusty road to Egypt. We had done everything man could do. Now it was in the Lord's hands."

At the plant things worsened. In a joint effort to ease the situation, every employee resigned. The company "rehired" those employees considered absolutely essential to the operation. Ralph's wife, Betty, worked the switchboard for a while, but it was not an easy job.

Then Ann took over. Although not eager for the task, Ann had personally met many of the creditors and dealers and had entertained some in their home. They would recognize her voice, Walt reasoned, and like the idea that the president's wife responded to their calls.

Sometimes she was able to answer questions or clear up misunderstandings without disturbing Walt. Other times she found out the nature of the call and alerted Walt so he could take a moment to pray for wisdom before answering the call.

Walt returned a newly purchased Lincoln car to the dealer and drove the old company pickup. Often the family walked instead of driving to demonstrate a willingness to adjust to the economic stress.

W.C. and Marion never went to court during the bankruptcy proceedings. Their sons chose to spare them the ordeal. But they could not escape the harassment day after day from anxious creditors. The family waited upon God for a solution.

"Our first answer," Walt says with characteristic candor, "was a gift of enough guts to get up and face the situation each day. And that was no small victory. God didn't give us comfort at that time, but He did give faith enough to face the next morning."

Though family assets were about even with liabilities, the trend appeared in the wrong direction. It seemed impossible to continue.

Until a series of provisions temporarily eased the burden.

It started with a loan from a Norwegian business friend, Torry Mosvold, from the Mosvold Shipping Company. The family had met the Scandinavian boat magnate through a mutual friend, Gus Gustafson, who had left New York in the mid-fifties to become Correct Craft's comptroller. For many years, as a part of the boat shows in New York and Chicago, the Meloons had sponsored a breakfast for their boat friends, always with a Christian theme. Mosvold had come as a guest of Gustafson to hear evangelist Jack Wyrtzen address the crowd.

The loan bought them a little more time.

What could they expect next?

9

The Long Climb Back

The letter came from Pakistan written on paper that looked like newsprint. It had misspellings and crossed-out words. The writer was a retired Pakistani army major, Moodi Farouki. He asked for a price quotation on boats like those Correct Craft had built for the U.S. Army in 1951. The U.S. government, it seems, had given some of those boats to Pakistan.

Not anxious to add more problems to the growing turmoil, the Meloons filed the letter away unanswered. Why go halfway around the world, they reasoned, to seek a partial solution to their dilemma? They had enough problems close to home.

Several weeks later another letter came from Farouki.

"Would you please do me the courtesy of answering my previous correspondence?" he pleaded. This time Correct Craft replied immediately. That began a flurry of correspondence that culminated in a $139,000 contract from the government of Pakistan. The Meloons promptly shipped one of their rejected sixteen-foot plastic boats to Pakistan's minister of defense, with the notice that many others were available.

An order came back for 239 of the rejected boats!

Several days later, at 3:00 A.M., a call came from Pakistan.

"Hello," a voice said indistinctly. "I'm Moodi Farouki. We've been corresponding. What kind of people
are you?"

"What do you mean, what kind of people are we?"
Walt asked, unsure of the question's intent.

"The U.S. government has sent a man over here to
tell our minister of defense that you people are not honorable, and not to do business with you."

Walt thought a moment before he replied.

"Well, Moodi," he said, trying to hear the distant
voice, "I can't answer all your questions by phone, but I'll
be glad to correspond further with you. What is this going to mean?"

"My government is canceling those two contracts."

Walt and the rest of the family reeled from shock.
Friends in Norway had already sent an additional forty
thousand dollar loan. That had been spent. Now Pakistan
was canceling the contracts. Where would the firm turn
next?

"At the office the next morning," Walt says, "the ca-
ble on my desk confirmed the cancellation. Our comptroller and treasurer were completely upset and wanted
to stop production on the boats.

"I told them we were not going to stop. We had committed the bidding process on these boats to the Lord.
We had even passed up the first two bid dates and sub-
mitted our bid on a third and final date, at Pakistan's insistence. I felt God had intervened.

"When we had the first boat ready to test, the Pakistan government told us they would reinstate our original
contract for the six larger boats. But the reinstatement
failed to arrive in the mails.

"When we shipped the first large boat, we also decided to send ten smaller boats along.

"Ten days later we received the checks for all eleven
boats.

"We continued to ship truckload after truckload, as the boats were finished. Back came the checks, with no protest. In time the Pakistan Embassy paid for all 239 of the boats they had originally requested."

As a result, the company enjoyed a new lease on life, at least for a time. But there were still those early morning calls from creditors. "I learned much from these experiences," Walt says. "By no means were all the financial problems solved, but by this time we had learned to relax and trust God. A few years previously I would have found it difficult to spend fifteen minutes at a time in prayer. Now I was spending up to an hour or more each day on my knees. We continued to work, and to pay a few more creditors, as the cash flow allowed."

Bud Coleman, owner of a local automobile agency, who had granted Correct Craft a loan on the plant property for ten years, provided another blessing. When the Meloons finally decided they could pay off the loan, Coleman refused to compound the interest. He simply had added each yearly amount of interest to the principle. Correct Craft was amazed.

And A. B. Johnson, founder of Orlando's best known electrical firm, and an associate in the Christian Businessmen's Committee of Orlando, also figured into God's plan. Although completely blind, Johnson had unusual abilities. In an occasional golf game together, Johnson would often shoot in the eighties. When Correct Craft had to build a badly needed warehouse, despite their financial straits, Johnson entered a ridiculously low bid on the wiring, with a deliberate strategy in mind.

Johnson knew that doing that would entitle him to attend the creditors' meetings, often when none of the Meloons had been invited. So Johnson "scouted" the meetings for them and looked after their best interests. His wise counsel over a period of many months kept the Meloon family from being forced out of the firm's management. A. B. Johnson, beloved among many central Floridians, turned out to be "the blind Samaritan."

"I came to love that man about as much as anyone on earth," Walt says. When A. B. Johnson died, his oldest son, Bob, called Walt early in the morning.

"Dad got his eyesight back today," he said.

While no one with any sense would ask for the experience of near-bankruptcy, its pressures seemed to draw the family into a well-knit unit. Earlier family tensions, not unknown even among the Meloons, seemed to vanish.

The next crisis taught a lesson in God's timing.

As bankruptcy proceedings dragged on, creditors called for a hearing in Tampa to have the Meloon family removed from the company's management. This time loss of the firm seemed imminent. The day in federal court arrived. A. B. Johnson insisted on riding from Orlando in the car with the Meloons, rather than with other members of the creditors' committee. Attorney Jim Welch and company controller Ray White also joined.

On the way to court they prayed in the car. "Lord, we know the charges are largely true. We have made mistakes. We need about forty-five days to get the problems straightened out."

In court that day the attorney for the creditors injected what he saw as a strong point for his case to oust the family once and for all.

"The Meloon family distributed ten thousand dollars among their creditors," he complained, "and didn't even tell me anything about it."

The judge listened, then stiffened noticeably, his face flushed. He had been the one who had signed the checks in question!

"It isn't necessary for you to be told what was done," the judge responded gruffly. "The court gave the order to do this."

Then he took his gavel and pounded on the desk.

"I'll be prepared to hear more on the Correct Craft matter on March 15 in Orlando," he said.

In the car going home, one of the men suddenly thought to count the number of days before the next hearing. They had prayed for forty-five.

There were forty-six!

The day of the next hearing in Orlando arrived. Correct Craft still had no solution to the firm's financial problems.

The opening move by the creditors' attorney caught them completely by surprise.

"Judge, I don't know why, but since the hearing in Tampa my clients have asked that I withdraw the complaints," he said.

In three minutes the hearing ended. Another important skirmish had been won. Yet negotiations dragged on for six more years. Finally, the judge retired, and the court appointed a replacement.

He promptly notified the family that he was going to liquidate the company in ten days.

By this time the small creditors had been paid off— 101 of them. They had all received 100 percent of what Correct Craft owed them.

A letter to the remaining 127 creditors asked a direct question: "Would you accept a settlement of 10 percent from the Meloon family within six months, in lieu of the judge putting us out of business?"

All but one creditor agreed. The judge contacted each creditor on his own to confirm the consensus. Satisfied, he released Correct Craft from Chapter 11 of the Bankruptcy Act on the first business day of 1965.

"Only a few weeks later," Walt says, "the government attorneys called our attorney, offering us a settlement of $40,000 if we would sign off on our original complaint. Admission by the government of fault revived the balance of our claim as a valid loss, totaling $280,000. The write-off would allow us to operate up to four years without paying any income tax, assuming profits did not exceed $280,000."

The Meloons accepted the forty thousand dollars and passed it on to creditors. Instead of a 10 percent settlement with the large creditors, the firm actually made a 5 percent payment, then followed it up with a 10 percent payment, then another 5 percent payment. That totaled 20 percent—twice what the court had directed. It more than satisfied the law.

But as time passed, it still did not satisfy the Meloons.

10

From the Fish's Mouth

Before 1984, Correct Craft had repaid all but $147,000 of its debt. Most of the businesses that had not been paid in full wrote off the balance to bad debt and forgot about it. Some former creditors now were dead. But at the outset of this particular year, the Meloons vowed with new determination to pay back the rest, even though they did not know where the money would come from.

They trusted God that this would be their "hallelujah year."

"The firm was still operating on borrowed capital, and banks do not make loans to corporations that are losing money," says Ralph, chairman of the board. "This meant that each time we paid five thousand dollars to a former creditor, we also had to set aside five thousand dollars for taxes (we were in a 48 percent bracket). So to come out even, we knew we would have to make about $300,000 more than usual in order to pay off the balance and taxes too.

"By May 1 we had whittled the balance down to fifty thousand dollars, though not without struggle. We also knew that by July 1 the new 1985 boat models would be ready, involving additional outlay for tooling and other related expenses. Our historical cash flow patterns told us that if we were to pay off all our debts, we'd have to see it happen by June.

"Now as background, Correct Craft sponsors a water-ski team with some of the best talent on U.S. and even world waters. It is good promotion for us. We pay these skiers monthly and provide their boats. It has helped spread the name of Correct Craft and our Ski Nautique far and wide.

"We also sponsor a bass fishing team. We provide a Bass Nautique. They fish in bass tournaments throughout the Southeast against thousands of excellent fishermen. But we pay them nothing. If they win any prize money, they get to keep half, and they give Correct Craft the other half."

The team had never won any big money.

Until one week in May 1984 during Super Bass III.

That week in world tournament competition, team member Doug Gilley fished off the south docks in Jacksonville's Naval Yard and down river by Lake George. In four days he pulled in more than fifty-three pounds of bass (limit seven fish a day) and won the world prize—$100,000!

The bass team received fifty thousand dollars, and Correct Craft received the other half, just enough to pay off the rest of the money it owed creditors.

Correct Craft and the Meloon family rejoiced and gave thanks to the Lord. And then they remembered a familiar event in the Scriptures.

Jesus had trekked to Capernaum, on the Sea of Galilee. There some of Jesus' critics asked Peter, "Doesn't your master pay taxes?"

When Peter asked Jesus, He replied, "Go down to the shore and throw in a line, and open the mouth of the first fish you catch. You will find a coin to cover the taxes for both of us; take it and pay them" (Matthew 17:24, 27).

"God had provided our last fifty thousand dollars," says Ralph, "out of the fish's mouth."

"God sees the end from the beginning," he insists. "The God who 'owns the cattle upon a thousand hills' could have orchestrated our solvency years ago, but we were not yet ready for it. There were too many things we still had to learn. The Lord knew what we needed, and also what the firm's next generation needed. This business belongs to Him."

Walt added, "The story of Moses' forty years in the wilderness didn't mean a thing to me until we spent years wandering under the cloud of bankruptcy. It was not the shortest route, but God has His purposes." In retrospect, some of those purposes already seem clear.

After receiving the fifty thousand dollar fishing prize, Correct Craft promptly sent out checks to the rest of its creditors, and with them copies of this book's original edition, *Saved from Bankruptcy.*

Firms responded with surprise, amazement, even disbelief. They commended the Meloons for their Christian convictions and integrity. Company presidents from Oshkosh to Boston, from Pittsburgh to Atlanta, from Baltimore to Orlando, wrote comments like these:

"There are probably no people we can think of who would give consideration in such an honorable fashion."

"It gives me a great faith in humanity to see someone like yourself step forth and pay an honest incurred debt."

"I was flabbergasted to learn that someone remembered an obligation that goes back twenty-five years. Many of the people working here today were mere youngsters at that time, and some are so young as to have not even been born."

It was not easy to find all the creditors. Some, in fact, were dead, and the check had to be delivered to an heir.

Ralph spent months trying to run down by phone an old creditor in Bloomfield Hills, near Detroit. Finally he flew there to conduct the search on site, only to find the man was deceased. At least one wrong party with the same name whom he befriended in the search, became an instant admirer of Correct Craft.

The impact of the Meloon bankruptcy story lives on through the thousands of copies of *Saved from Bankruptcy* that were received by Correct Craft boat owners (the book came with the warranty) and the public at large.

Meanwhile, Walt and Ralph were telling the story to groups around the world, even years before the debt was totally paid off. Walt first told it publicly to missionaries on the south coast of West Irian, Indonesia, who needed fifty thousand dollars to replace a hospital that had washed into the sea. Repeating the thought that "God is not poor," Walt inspired them to trust their Lord for the money. In the next two years $100,000 came in.

The story appeared in *CBMC Contact* (April 1968), in *Power* magazine (August 9, 1970), and later in *Guideposts* (November 1973). The latter article stemmed from an introduction to a New York couple, new Christians and owners of a Correct Craft, who at the time were teetering on the verge of bankruptcy. For three days the Meloons counseled and prayed with Ernie and Ruth Jones, who in turn contacted Richard H. Schneider, then senior editor of *Guideposts.* The magazine sent an editor to Orlando to research the story. More recently, features have appeared both in *Moody Monthly* and in Billy Graham's *Decision* magazine.

One result of the Meloon's concern for helping the financially troubled has been Correct Craft-sponsored retreats at Camp-of-the-Woods, in the New York Adirondacks, and Hidden Lake, in northern Georgia, for people facing financial disaster.

Hardworking people, just like the Meloons, have similar stories.

A farmer from Iowa shares his financial burdens. He has 1,600 acres of farm land, raising grain and hogs. Bad weather has plagued him two years in a row. Agricultural financing has tightened. Meanwhile, imports from Canada

and Denmark have helped deflate prices. There may be
no way out but to sell the farm that has been in the family
for decades.

An Indiana couple face bankruptcy, forced by a bank
that closed its doors and by the suicide of the prime financial offender. "One of our greatest needs," the couple
admits, "is to be willing and able to forgive those who
were unfair. Those responsible for our financial difficulty."

A Georgia construction company owner and his wife
have just walked through both corporate and personal
bankruptcy. "God's grace is sufficient," they conclude.

A Texan with the reputation as a good manager, never
before in financial difficulty, says how good it is to be
among people who really care. "I have people I owe
money to and I really want to pay them, but I can't."

A Nebraskan, who came close to bankruptcy four
years previously, tells others at the retreat: "Don't let
poverty or self-sufficiency rob you of the joy of the mirac-
ulous. And in recovery, don't forget to thank God."

These people return home to face the future with
new hope and perspective. The problems are still there,
but somehow they now seem less formidable.

The Georgia couple are making headway. "The wife
is now teaching school," says Walt, "and the husband is
running a washer appliance business. They have also
added a business in English antiques. They are making
headway on their debts. A year ago they thought bankruptcy inevitable."

The Iowa farmer has an even greater story.

"While flying across Iowa," says Walt, "we dropped
in and had lunch with him. They had owned a farm worth
millions. During the flush in the farm economy they borrowed against it from the government, who in turn val-
ued it way up by the acre. A year later the crops were
bad and the economy deteriorated. The government then

devalued the property and wanted hundreds of thousands of dollars back. The farmer didn't have it, so they took the farm away from him and sold it.

"But that's not the end of the story.

"The new owner promptly offered the farmer a lease, with option to buy his farm back at reasonable interest. That's how God worked in his case."

But not all bankruptcy is financial, Walt insists. "God has used bankruptcy ever since the Garden of Eden. There was bankruptcy with Adam and Eve, not in dollars and cents, but total bankruptcy of discipline to do God's will when Cain killed Abel. David repeatedly faced bankruptcy. When Moses killed the Egyptian he had to run for the desert. All of their experiences had the same elements found in financial bankruptcy.

"Divorce is nothing but a bankruptcy of love and affection. I believe God wants to handle all bankruptcy in the same way."

Ironically, from Correct Craft's darkest hours also came two key business decisions that set the stage for the firm's current success.

At that time company officials decided to set up five factory warehouse distribution centers in scattered areas of the United States. Family members operated most of them. These autonomous centers, first of their kind in the boating industry, proved successful in selling Correct Craft boats to dealers in their areas, tapping new markets, and generating income.

The other key move involved a newfangled kind of boat that founder W.C. almost refused to make.

11

No Fiberglass Trees

Back in 1959, bankruptcy seemed imminent. Yet late in the year an event occurred that would be significant in making the company the success it is today. Jim Harmon, writing in *Powerboat* magazine, tells the story:

"Late in 1959 a Miami ski school operator named Leo Bentz came to the Correct Craft Boat Company in Pine Castle, Fla., hoping to make a deal. Bentz had designed what he called the greatest water ski towboat ever, and he made a sales pitch to correct Craft's then executive vice president and chief designer, Walter O. Melloon. The new boat's molds were for sale for $10,000.

"Without hesitating, Meloon made it clear to Bentz that his company wasn't interested. For one thing, Correct Craft was in the midst of what often appeared—at least to outsiders—as a losing battle against bankruptcy. " 'I knew Leo, but I had no idea of buying his boat,' W.O. remembers. 'At that point we couldn't have paid $10,000 for anything.'

"Aside from Correct Craft's financial troubles, there were other reasons for the rejection of Bentz's proposal. "The boat was made of fiberglass, the mere mention of which made company founder Walter C. Meloon, W.O.'s father, fume. The elder Meloon's aversion to the new material stemmed partly from the company's first foray into fiberglass technology—a government contract made two years earlier for 3,000 such boats—which had left Correct Craft in its financial bind. Even though the switch to fiberglass wasn't the actual culprit, the new technology was guilty by association.

And Bentz was hardly the sophisticated, well-financed boating entrepreneur. . . . His ski school business, similar to any functioning at the time, was run on a shoestring budget, and he had turned to designing boats to help support himself. . . .

"[Correct Craft's current president, Walter N. Meloon, cites another obstacle.] 'Bentz's pitch focused on tournament water skiing, and we had no idea what tournament water skiing was all about. We couldn't relate to the market.'

"Bentz was sent on his way, and that was that. Until a year later, that is, when he appeared in the boat company's lobby once again. 'If I remember correctly, this time we tried to ignore him, but he wouldn't go away,' laughs Walter N. And this time Bentz made no attempt to hide his desperation. His wife was about to have a baby, and he was now using the ski school to support his grind through law school. He was unable to fill the orders for ski boats fast enough, taking his molds to whatever builders would agree to throw two or three rigs together. Unfortunately, the boats which were in use were showing signs that 'thrown together' was exactly what they were.

" 'This time,' recalls W.O., 'Leo said, "I have got to get rid of this." He offered to *give* us the molds if we would fix the boats in the field and build him one a year for three years for his ski school. So we took him up on it.'

" 'If for no other reason than to get him off our backs,' adds W.N. 'Then, while we were testing one of his boats, we found out that it ran pretty well.'

"Happily, Bentz went on to finish law school, and the Meloons did OK, too. Today the Meloon/Correct Craft name is known to just about anyone who's interested in water skiing. Although W.C. is gone, Walter O., his brother Ralph and Walter N. have gone on to create the most widely used, easily recognized and arguably the best water ski tow boat in the history of the sport, the Ski Nautique. In the process they have done as much to promote organized waterskiing as anyone in the industry."[1]

Walt "oversaw the production of the new ski boats made from Bentz's molds," Harmon continues. But now he had to promote the boat in the marketplace. That meant he had to get some of them into tournaments. Harmon picks up the story:

"W.O. contacted Bill Clifford, executive director of the American Water Ski Association, for advice on how to go about promoting the new boat. 'He told me the skiers had to ask for it,' says W.O., who asked Clifford for a list of 15 of the top competitive skiers. He offered everyone on the list a new Ski Nautique at half price if they would use it and take it to tournaments. Fourteen of the fifteen took Correct Craft up on the deal, and tournament waterskiing hasn't been the same since.

" 'It's important to note that the sport was coming of age, and the Meloons were definitely in the right place at the right time,' says Clifford. 'Just as importantly, they *listened.* I think that's the success story.'

"The decision to offer the promotional boats to the skiers came at a time when the company's financial troubles were at their height. 'People within my own organization thought I was nuts,' W.O. says, 'because we were right on the edge of bankruptcy. But I guess there are just some things it's easier to apologize for than to get permission. Now we produce around 200 promotional boats a year, and I think that's had a lot to do with waterskiing's fast growth.' "[2]

But as Harmon notes, sometimes "even those within the company, most notably [W. C. Meloon, were] slow to change. . . . Especially when the subject was fiberglass

1. Jim Harmon, "The Meloons: Three Parts Know-How, Three Parts Faith," *Powerboat*, August 1982.
2. Ibid.

back in 1957." For a man reared on the qualities of wood, fiberglass wasn't easy for W.C. to accept. In his view, it even seemed to contradict the law of nature. As Walter N. put it, "according to W.C., there were no fiberglass trees, so that wasn't the way to go."[3]

Then how did the company convince him?

"We built the first fiberglass boat," says Walter N., "while W.C. was in New Hampshire at another warehouse, because he never would've allowed it if he were here. So we sent him one, with no explanation, and the truck driver said, 'Mr. Meloon, wait until you see the new fiberglass boat they've built.' We would've liked to have seen the look on his face."[4]

The success of Correct Craft is the result of other factors than the adoption of the fiberglass boat, as Harmon notes: "Correct Craft has had a continuing test and research program, especially with the Ski Nautique 2001. 'That was Dad's brainchild,' says Walter N. today. 'He came up with the idea, and that got the creative juices of all our design people flowing. We've kept the competitive skiers involved and used them to test the results of any changes we've made. We get suggestions from them as well as ideas from our own people.'

" 'We've spent a lot of money developing new ideas,' says Ralph of the company. 'Also, we've brought a lot of people up in the company, which is important.'

" 'And,' Ralph concludes, 'anything we've done that's been good has been with God's help.' "[5]

Ski Nautique 2001 made an exceptional debut in its first year in tournament use. It was the exclusive tow boat at the 24th Annual Masters Tournament and at the World Cup in London. It was used in all the regional ski

3. Ibid.
4. Ibid.
5. Ibid.

tournaments and at the Nationals, where Cory Pickos set a world trick record.

What makes it a favorite of skiers is the broad, flat wake it produces, which gives skiers a smooth ride.

Yet despite the fame of the Ski Nautique, Correct Craft had already established a reputation for quality and class. Robert G. Speltz, in a book called *The Runabouts,* says he was surprised to discover "the stylish-looking all-mahogany utilities the firm built prior to the start of World War II."

Correct Craft inboards appeared at Cypress Gardens about 1936. The untold exposure in the many shows there, says Speltz, "helped spread the name 'Correct Craft' nationwide, making it a common household word."

When World War II broke, the company turned to defense and built numerous pontoon boats for bridges, all from plywood. They also made boats for the Korean War. By 1952 the emphasis turned back to recreation, and the line that year even featured a super luxurious fifty-foot yacht, though few of them were ever built. In 1957, tailfins began to appear, along with wraparound windshields and two-tone paint jobs. The firm built its last true runabout in 1958—the eighteen-foot Collegian.

Today's market ranges from family boating to the professional skiing circuit. Because of the Meloon family's interest in the Christian movement among America's young people, their boats have long played a part in recreation at such places as Word of Life's Schroon Lake resort in the Adirondacks, at Camp-of-the-Woods near Speculator, New York, at Young Life in British Columbia, and at Wheaton College's Honey Rock Camp in Wisconsin.

With Correct Craft's surge into the top ranks of the water-ski world, however, has come remarkable opportunity to spread the gospel of Jesus Christ, not simply to professionals, but to a significant segment of today's outdoor-oriented young generation. In large part it's because of the Ski Nautique, despite the fact that W.C. didn't like it at first, and no one has yet found a fiberglass tree.

12
Water-Skiers and God

In October 1984, Mike Botti, a former national bare-footer water-ski champion and professional show skier at Sea World and Cypress Gardens, moved into a modest office at Correct Craft.

Botti was not expected to build boats or to sell them. In fact, he was not even an employee of Correct Craft, although they gave him his office rent free. Instead, he took his "corporate" signals from Kansas City and the national headquarters of the Fellowship of Christian Athletes (FCA).

The movement has long been prominent in the major sports, with Tom Landry, legendary coach of the Dallas Cowboys, as perhaps its foremost encourager. In more recent years the movement has also spilled over into other sports, such as rodeo, which got its boost after a Sunday morning cowboy service on horseback at the Cheyenne rodeo in 1973. Perhaps it was inevitable that sooner or later the movement would also find its way into the water-ski world.

It already involves hundreds, even thousands, of participants from world-class skiers down to the teenage crowds that turn out for FCA-sponsored water-ski sports camps, clinics, exhibitions, and fellowships. The movement publishes a newsletter called "Mainstream" and other materials to help spread the good news, including brochures such as "How to Organize a Morning Devotion at a Water Ski Tournament." Water-ski schools, such as the one operated by National Champion skiers Dave and Cyndi Benzel in Groveland, Florida, provide further Christian outreach.

Recently the Fellowship of Christian Athletes Water Ski Ministry released a water-ski video featuring several top-name professionals—among them Harold Cole, foremost name in freestyle skiing and a member of Correct Craft's Competition Ski Team. Cole has invented many of the popular tricks used in freestyle competition, and his friendly nature makes him one of the most popular skiers among his peers.

Cole was working out on the trampoline at Sea World on his Christmas vacation in 1984, when he miscalculated a double front flip and crashed on his head. Lying flat on his back, paralyzed from his shoulders down, he was rushed to the hospital. X-rays revealed a broken neck. Doctors said he might not walk again. Despite the somber prognosis, Cole found immediate peace in the many Scriptures he had memorized.

"While in intensive care," Cole recalls, "I gave my address book to one of the nurses, and she began to call my Christian friends all over the country to pray. At three o'clock in the morning I was praying for strength and praising God for the peace He had given me. All of a sudden I felt a warmth come over me, and for the first time since jumping on the trampoline I had movement and feeling in my whole body. God in His infinite grace had healed me. I yelled at the top of my lungs, 'Praise the Lord!' With that, five nurses rushed to my bed."

The doctors still insisted on surgery. Cole walked on his own two days after the operation and was released thirteen days after suffering the broken neck, both feats setting hospital records. In the FCA-produced video "Living Waters," Cole appears in top form.

"Living Waters" features some of the best waterskiing footage ever seen, including multiple ramp flips, the 720-degree helicopter spin, the Mobius strip, trick ski wake gainers, long distance jumping, hot barefoot action, doubles, and more. But the most unique aspect of the video is the skiers' personal testimonies of their faith in Jesus Christ.

Among those featured, besides Cole, are Scott Green, former National Men's I overall champion; Lori Powell, World Champion Barefooter; Sea World's Andy Hansen; Cypress Gardens skiers Jimmy Cassata and Jeannie Baier; and Mike Botti. Former Masters champion Frankie Dees and Cypress Gardens skier Phil Baier also perform. The dramatic ten-minute footage has already helped introduce the sport of waterskiing, and the gospel, to thousands.

While the 1984 launch of FCA's National Water Ski Ministry gave new impetus to the Christian movement in this sport, an informal fellowship already existed. Ralph cites Mike Suyderhoud of Redding, California, as the first person to become interested in starting a Fellowship of Christian Water Skiers as far back as the early 1970's. Suyderhoud asked the American Water Ski Association to publish word of his vision and to ask any potential organizers to write to him. He received about one hundred responses—too many for him to follow up personally. "Mike talked to Correct Craft about the problem," Ralph says, "and we decided to take his list of names and try to build a larger mailing list." Within a few years the list grew to two hundred names.

"The American Water Ski Federation," adds Ralph, "allowed us to use Friday night at each national championship as our special meeting night. We had some exceptionally good speakers, among them former astronaut Jim Irwin. We have also had good cooperation from magazines such as *Spray* and *World Water Skiing*."

Each morning Correct Craft customer service manager John Gillette meets with others to pray for the Christian water-ski movement. Gillette, too, has been "one of them."

One of the most respected names in waterskiing, Gillette was a founding member of the American Barefoot Club (ABC) and a competitor in two world championships in 1978 (Australia) and 1980 (San Francisco). As chairman of the ABC Rules Committee, Gillette initiated many of the progressive refinements to the rules. He wrote the highly acclaimed *John Gillette's Complete Guide to Barefoot Water Skiing* in 1981 and has served as a technical advisor and contributing writer to *Water Ski Magazine* and *World Water Skiing* for many years. A former member of Correct Craft's Competition Ski Team, he appeared in many exhibitions and boat shows on their behalf and assisted in the design and testing of Barefoot Nautique, waterskiing's only bona fide competition barefoot boat.

In 1980 Gillette, as he describes it, was "big man on site" at the barefoot waterskiing tournaments around the country—heading for the world championships, a winner in Europe, president of the American Barefoot Club. In fact, he became known as "the Barefooter's Barefooter."

But in 1981 at Sea World of Ohio, he found himself isolated from consistent tournament practice. Meanwhile, the competition became more fierce than ever. Barefooting had grown, and many young skiers were out to make a name for themselves in the sport. Some were beating him. Gillette had not learned a new trick in two years. Driving to the Nationals, he foresaw humiliation. Almost thoughtlessly, he flipped a cassette into his tape deck. It was by a gifted young singer named Amy Grant. She was singing a song written by Gary Chapman, "All I Ever Have to Be:

> When the weight of all my dreams
> Are resting heavy on my head,
> And the thoughtful words of help and hope
> Have all been nicely said,
> But I'm still hurtin', wonderin if I'll ever
> Be the one I think I am. And You gently
> Re-remind me that You made me from the first.

And the more I try to be the best,
The more I get the worst.
And I realize the good in me is only there
Because of who You are. You made me.
Any more or less would be a step out of
Your plan. . . . And all I ever have to be
Is what You made me.[1]

Gillette's attention promptly turned from his own self-pride to the God of the universe. "The words of David in Psalm 46," he says, "rang out in my heart: 'God is our refuge and strength, a tested help in times of trouble. . . . Stand silent! Know that I am God!' "

In the competition that followed, Gillette enjoyed a highly successful performance.

1.   Gary Chapman, "All I Ever Have to Be." Paragon Music Corporation, Nashville, Tennessee.

13

The Making of a Magazine

Company publications are a dime a dozen, so it's not unusual that the Meloons would have one. But the *Correct Craft Tribune* is no ordinary magazine.

Once a newsprint tabloid called the *Orlando Tribune,* it is now a slick, forty-page magazine with full-color covers, advertising, and state-of-the-art graphic design packed with industry news. Every four months an issue goes out to at least 100,000—including 65,000 individual subscribers. The other copies are distributed through dealers and at tournaments, boat shows, clinics, and other promotional events. Each press run costs some forty thousand dollars. No other boat company in the world goes to this expense to reach its "family" of owners and other enthusiasts.

Its most unusual feature, however, has been its prominent Christian content. Over the years the byline of evangelist Billy Graham has appeared almost regularly in the magazine, and its pages often carry news of his crusades. An issue seldom goes out without a devotional feature. The water-ski ministry receives generous coverage, and sometimes sprinkled throughout the magazine's letters to the editor columns are reactions to the magazine's spiritual content.

Do the readers object?

At least one man from Florida did, and the magazine printed his complaint in full. In part it read:

When one decides to go public with their religious beliefs, they place themselves at the same risk as the current glut of electronic preachers; i.e., they are perceived as nothing more than pious, self-righteous, mealy-mouthed hypocrites. But even worse than that is the nearly terminal boredom induced by the never-ending affirmations of faith.

I will hasten to assure you that I will in the future avoid your publication like the plague.

But such letters are extremely uncommon. Instead, literally scores of readers write each year commending the magazine for its spiritual and moral stance. Letters such as this one are typical in almost every issue:

I have just received my Fall copy of the *Tribune,* and it is fantastic. I couldn't put it down until I read it from cover to cover. I really appreciate the Christian oriented articles and the stand your company takes for Christ! I am an avid water skier and have been skiing the lakes of central and northern Indiana for the past fifteen years. As of yet I do not own a Ski Nautique, but by the start of the next ski season I hope to have one.

And in the same issue these two letters appeared:

I am a Christian attorney practicing law in Surfside Beach, South Carolina. I received my first copy of the *Tribune* today and was most inspired to learn that Correct Craft Inc. is a Christian corporation managed by God-fearing men.

How grateful I am that I filled out a card at Sea World this past summer to learn about Ski Nautique. I got on the mailing list for the *Correct Craft Tribune* and have become most appreciative of the tremendous Christian witness you have.

As one who spent almost two decades in public education in teaching and coaching, and as one still involved in coaching Babe Ruth baseball, I am interested in young people; we have taught some 200 to water ski on Lake Jordan here in Alabama over the years. I am involved in the Fellowship of Christian Athletes and it is good to see the name of FCA often in your publication. Continue to build the best boat that money can buy—but above all, continue to carry the message of Jesus Christ wherever you go.

"Thanks for the *Tribune*," reads another letter. "It is like reading my Sunday school lesson. I am 75 and still ski a little—never won a medal or a trophy. On August 3 you will see me on National TV as I get crowned 'King of Hobos' at the National Hobo Convention in Iowa." It was signed "Rudy Phillips." *Tribune* readers literally come from all walks of life.

The *Tribune* originated with Norm Sewell, the Pennsylvania executive who joined the firm in 1951. Almost from the start, Sewell promoted the idea of a house organ, but it was 1958 before the first issue came off the press. By 1970 it announced its goal to become the largest circulated publication in the industry. Sewell edited the publication for a number of years, until it was turned over to Walter N., now company president. In later years Harvey McLeod was editor, until Sue McMurray, a recent graduate of Michigan State University, became editor in the spring of 1986. Sue is a tournament water-skier in her own right and a member of the American Water Ski Association.

Back issues of the *Tribune* feature a number of noteworthy stories and items on Correct Craft promotion.

In 1976, stock car racer Cale Yarborough, friend of Walter N., was given a sparkling new 1976 Ski Nautique for winning the Atlanta 500. Yarborough and his family spent many summer hours skiing behind this competition tow boat at their lake house on the Santee Cooper in South Carolina. In 1985 he turned it in to Correct Craft for a new Ski Nautique 2001.

In October 1985, Michael Cash, a police officer from San Diego, won a Ski Nautique 2001 on "The Price Is

Right." Three months later Sandra Jones of Kentucky won a Bass Nautique on the same television show.

On television newscasts and national shows, including "Real People," viewers have seen Twiggy the waterskiing squirrel. She skis behind her own miniature size Ski Nautique. The thirty-inch boat is powered by an electric motor and is fully radio controlled with forward and reverse. "Twig's Rig" boasts top speed of approximately twenty miles per hour, although Twiggy prefers a more leisurely speed. Trainer Chuck Best of Sanford, Florida, takes Twiggy to boat fairs and boat shows, along with the smallest craft the firm has ever built, and now the squirrel even hang glides. Correct Craft enjoys the promotion, but Twiggy didn't make the best first impression when her trainer first introduced her and the idea of a waterskiing squirrel to Correct Craft officials in their Orlando offices. She bit Walter N. on the ear!

Now Best has introduced Chips, the waterskiing horse, who made his nationwide television debut recently on "That's Incredible." Chips uses a full-size Ski Nautique and skis in the "people position" with his front feet elevated on a bar twelve inches high. He voluntarily mounts the ski platform at the edge of the water, then maintains that position while being towed across the lake, mane and tail flying in the breeze. As the boat makes several turns, Chips stays in position, occasionally shifting his weight to accommodate the turns.

Sometimes Chips loses his balance, falls off his skis, and has to swim to shore. Then, just like any other skier, he shakes off the water and waits for the boat to come back and give him another pull.

But now it's Best's poodle, seen regularly in the introductory film footage of CNN news, that has the greatest exposure.

The *Correct Craft Tribune* reports the visits of interesting people to the plant—like the mayor of Orlando, or crack pilots from the Blue Angels, or Brother Andrew, who has spent much of his life smuggling Bibles into the Communist world.

During Brother Andrew's visit he asked Ralph if Bibles could be stowed in Correct Crafts going to Russia. "He was trying to get me to put my faith where my mouth was," says Ralph. "But when I sent him photos of a Ski Nautique, he was unable to figure out how to make compartments that would be able to hide the Bibles."

Chuck Colson visited the Correct Craft plant in 1979 while in Orlando for the mayor's prayer breakfast. The *Tribune* took its entire front page and several columns inside to carry the dramatic story of Colson's conversion. In that same issue, Tom Moses, general manager, Reedy Creek Improvement District, Walt Disney World, wrote a full-page Bible exposition titled "Through Troubled Waters."

It is not unusual for contributors to the magazine's devotional pages to pick up on the jargon of the boating world. One writer found an analogy in the boat trailer hitch: "We are oft-times more concerned with the proper connection between vehicle and trailer," he writes, "than we are the proper connection between life today and life eternal."

The writer refers to Jesus' words to "launch out into the deep," and alludes to such qualities as security ("And I give eternal life to them, and they shall never perish," John 10:28, NASB*) and trailability ("Jesus said . . . , 'If you wish to be complete . . . come, follow Me," Matthew 19:21, NASB).

Among all the visitors to the Correct Craft plant, none was more colorful than former Peruvian headhunter Chief Tariri, who ventured out into the civilized world in 1965. The *Tribune* told his remarkable story in several pages of photo and text.

*New American Standard Bible.

In the next few chapters, we will join the Meloon family traveling on the continents and see how God has used them in remarkable international situations.

14
The Ski Nautique
and the Family Mystique

When W. C. Meloon founded his small boat company near Orlando more than sixty years ago, he could not have foreseen the firm's impact upon the decades ahead. His boats would someday skim the waters of the world and help spread water-ski sports among millions. This very sport would open remarkable doors to proclaim the gospel. Moreover, two of his three sons—Ralph and Walt—would shuttle from Orlando into the nations of the world, proclaiming not only the merits of their boats but also the merits of their Savior.

Correct Craft is the oldest and one of the largest boat firms in the United States to remain family owned and operated.

The family would be the first to admit that it is far from perfect. Tensions occasionally do surface, as they did for a time when Walt was out of the country for extended periods with evangelist Billy Graham, and others had to assume the extra load in the firm's day-to-day operations. Like many Christian families, they sometimes worry about the younger generation and how well they'll maintain the spiritual climate established by the older generation.

W. C. Meloon served as president of the company he founded for thirty years. In 1955, Ralph assumed that role. Six years later Walt stepped in as president, and Ralph became chairman of the board.

Behind the scenes, however, a third brother, Harold, played a significant role, although he never aspired to the ranks of high management within the company. Instead, he preferred to work with his hands and serve as a consultant and company chaplain.

Harold started flying a glider at the age of twelve. "We used to have wonderful times barnstorming all over the country," he says. "All of us flew the primary glider behind high-speed boats, even Dad."

Harold inherited from his father both a humorous and a serious nature, and Harold's own sons often call him the family jester. He learned boatbuilding skills early. At age fourteen he was building two rowboats a day in the plant, for which his dad paid him $2.50 apiece and twenty-five cents to paint them. That was a lot of money for a teenager in those days.

By the time he was seventeen, Harold was handling a crew of men in Winter Park as they put retaining walls down through the canal system. Like his brothers, he learned valuable lessons of discipline and work at a young age.

His expertise as a machinist, tool-and-die maker, welder, and designer made him a valuable adviser at the plant. In his early twenties, as plant engineer, he designed and installed boat trailers, overhead cranes, and boat dollies. During World War II, when Correct Craft built pontoon boats for bridges, they had to be handled manually. Harold believed he could come up with a better method. His father had doubts. Buying an old car for thirty dollars, Harold and a friend stripped it and built a crane. It saved a lot of time and manpower, and Correct Craft still uses its counterparts today.

In 1945 Harold started his own business, Southern Metal Fabricating Company, a quarter mile down the road from the Correct Craft plant. He built playground equipment for parks and schools and boat trailers for Correct Craft. Later he sold the property to Correct Craft, and today it is the site of the firm's trailer plant.

In 1974 Harold assumed a new calling, that of minister of visitation for his church. But early on Monday mornings he can be found at Correct Craft leading the weekly prayer meeting. The prayer group is a cross section of two generations, but the men are united in spirit and earnest in their prayers. One senses that here, perhaps, is where the genius of the company really lies.

As recently as 1985, Walt retired as president of the company his dad had founded, although he remains co-chairman of the board. Walt's son, Walter N., became president, the third generation to hold this position. He had formerly been vice president/general manager.

Walter N. began working at Correct Craft's Lake Tyler sales office in 1955. Except for five years with the Martin Company, he had been a driving force in the growth of Correct Craft. Walter N. is one of the most respected individuals involved in the organized sport of waterskiing. He has served as president of the American Water Ski Educational Foundation. At Correct Craft he has surrounded himself with a solid management team.

Correct Craft has been the leader of inboard competition water-ski boats since 1961. The new president wants to hold that advantage and build on it. In 1986 the company celebrated the twenty-fifth anniversary of the Ski Nautique. Correct Craft rewrote the rules on state-of-the-art boats in 1981 when it introduced the Ski Nautique 2001. Its variable planing hull performs perfectly at all speeds and has proven to be the most preferred tow boat of competitors. In 1985 the firm introduced a twenty-foot bowrider, the Martinique. It has all the comfort and appointments the recreational boater could expect.

When Correct Craft first released the Ski Nautique, it knew little about the professional water-ski circuit. Today Walter N. knows it well. Although sometimes called "Lit-

tle Walt" to distinguish him from his father, he towers
six-foot four-inches. Young Walt majored in mischief
through several of his formative years. At six years old,
while painting the inside of a boat, he dutifully painted
the face of a workman who suddenly appeared in front of
him.

Walter N. remembers his grandfather as one who
also acted on impulse. "One Thanksgiving he decided he
wanted every Correct Craft family to have a turkey. He
went out and bought a truckload of the fowl, then distributed them to some three hundred employees at the Titusville and Pine Castle plants."

During his teenage years, the new president of Correct Craft spent five years under the Christian influence
of Hampden-DuBose Academy in Zellwood, Florida. He
remembers receiving Christ as his Savior at a little Baptist church in Titusville, under the ministry of Reverend
Ben Hall.

Although the presidency has passed from father to
son, Ralph C. remains as chairman of the board. His
brother, Walter O., is secretary and treasurer of the
Board. On February 4, 1986, the board lost its senior officer. That day Marion Meloon, wife of Correct Craft's
founder W.C., died at ninety-three. A tribute from the
family on her behalf in the *Correct Craft Tribune* (Spring
1986) concluded: "Although we grieve her passing, we
are thankful for her loving memory and the Christian leg-
acy she leaves behind."

During Correct Craft's years of bankruptcy and financial crisis, the company reorganized and established
six regional territories for sales and distribution, a move
that has proved successful. Midwest Correct Craft has
prospered in sales. Much of the credit goes to Ken Meloon, youngest son of Ralph, who has directed the Midwest operation since 1974 from Angola, Indiana. The
small town is tucked away in the northeast corner of the
state, amid many recreational lakes. Ken, his wife,

Diane, and their children, Greg and Mindy, live in the nearby town of Auburn.

Ken has worked faithfully to build the Midwest territory and has managed it wisely. A man of deep spiritual commitment, he is serving in a Bible-believing local church and seeks to glorify God with the resources the Lord has bountifully supplied through the business. He echoes his father's conviction that God honors those who honor Him. There is great joy, he is convinced, in being a part of God's plan of spreading the gospel of Jesus Christ to a lost world.

Ralph, Jr., Ken's older brother, is president of Pacific Coast Correct Craft. He shuttles between corporate offices near Sacramento and his home in Soldotna, Alaska. Walt's son-in-law, Robert Warner, manages Correct Craft's New England warehouse in Rochester, New Hampshire.

Bob and Etta Warner, in fact, reside in the very region of New England where W. C. Meloon launched his career. In that corner of the United States the boating season is short, but little lakes abound. One bright winter day they took me by car to trace the family's roots.

Our excursion took us first to the old family farm tucked away on a back country road near Province Lake, hugging the Maine border. From there we circled back to Ossipee and past the cottages W.C. had built on Duncan Lake, which the family calls "New England's first motel." Although now more than sixty years old, the little cottages sparkled with fresh red paint against a two-foot backdrop of snow that had fallen days earlier. For Etta, the landmarks brought back childhood memories.

Even the Warner home seemed to capture the family's rich pioneer heritage—a large century-old chest in the living room, a thick fireplace mantel board, an old sugar bucket, a colonial rifle, a prominent family portrait. Three Meloon brothers had sailed the southern shores of England and settled in the New World, at least one of them near Portsmouth, New Hampshire. Whether they were among those who helped transplant the name *Portsmouth* from that well-known maritime city on the English Channel to the shores of New England, the Meloons never seemed to live far from the sea.

Correct Craft did not establish its New England office until 1971, when it assigned Bob Warner, formerly with Martin-Marietta and then Correct Craft's purchasing agent, to that region. The Warner family has thoroughly enjoyed the land that earlier Meloons had known so well. Oldest son Craig has remained there as the region's parts and service manager. His brother Jeff works at the plant in Orlando.

As I watched Craig refinish a boat left in their repair shop by a New England owner, he pointed out to me some of the refinements of the Correct Craft product, including a unique personal touch: the owner's nameplate mounted to the dash.

Other Meloons of the third generation are with the company at plant level, including two of Harold's sons: Steve, company test pilot and troubleshooter (who also maintains the boats at Sea World), and youngest son Dan, a department foreman at the trailer plant. Eric Abel, son of Ralph's daughter Marion, is foreman of hardware and trim.

Now even some of the fourth generation are involved in the operation. Gary Meloon, son of company president Walter N., has been supervising night-shift production. His sister Lori Ann works at the new sales office of Southeast Correct Craft, a mile from the main plant. Both have recently married.

Today a gathering of the Meloon family, now going into its fifth generation, is an impressive crowd. For the past several Christmases, many family members have gathered at Camp-of-the-Woods in the Adirondacks. It is not only a family social retreat, but a chance to spiritually recharge before the start of a new year. The company's management team has also gathered there for business and management seminars. For some, Camp-of-the-Woods brings back special memories. Says Gary Meloon, "I met my wife there while working at the camp during summers."

Correct Craft has long had a close association with another major Christian retreat site in the Adirondacks —evangelist Jack Wyrtzen's Word of Life ministry at Schroon Lake. Wyrtzen's youngest son, Ron, is Correct Craft's sales representative for its Mid-Atlantic region. (Ron's wife, Christine, is a nationally known gospel singer and his older brother, Don, one of the nation's foremost Christian composers/arrangers.)

For the Meloons there is a rich family heritage to pass on, although each offspring in time has to make his own decisions, even about the Christian faith. Those decisions affect the future. W.C. was a prime example of how one single life can help shape the lives of others for good and even impact generations to come. Perhaps a verse in Psalms best makes the point: "Let each generation tell its children what glorious things he does" (Psalm 145:4).

15
Earthquakes, Jungle Chiefs, and Fire Canoes

February 4, 1976. Guatemalans go about life as usual. Suddenly the earth roars, and the ground underneath heaves. Roads crack. Bricks fall. Houses tumble; some even disappear from the face of the earth. Within minutes more than twenty thousand Guatemalans are dead or fatally injured.

The earthquake registers 7.5 on the Richter scale. Much of the countryside lies in devastation, including many of its evangelical churches. Residents who have survived begin the clean-up. Much of the outside world reads the newspaper reports, sympathizes, but sees little it can do about the tragedy.

Not Walt Meloon.

At the time he was president of the men's movement within the Christian and Missionary Alliance church, a denomination with deep roots in world missions. These were men sensitive to events abroad. Among them were men of many talents, including construction skills. Why not challenge the men, Walt reasoned, to help rebuild the homes and churches of Guatemala?

Walt contacted denomination officials. The word went out to laymen. Within four days, as a way of assisting in the reconstruction, they had dispatched to Guatemala twenty-five machines used in the rapid manufacture of cement blocks. Guatemalan Christians made thousands of blocks and stacked them to await the end of the rainy season.

Meanwhile, in the States, men everywhere responded. The Christian and Missionary Alliance church organized teams of thirty to forty men each, who rotated to Guatemala on a two-week basis, at their own expense. Harold Meloon also went to Guatemala to help. The first groups assembled in Miami and San Francisco. These were not wealthy men, merely ordinary men whose hearts had been touched by the Lord. They met in the airline terminals with hammers and saws, levels and plumb bobs.

Their first priority was Tecpan, a village of thirty thousand located about ninety minutes by winding road from the nation's capital. Three thousand had died there, including three of the town's five evangelical pastors, and one hundred from the Central American Mission's congregation.

Excited, wide-eyed national church leaders looked on in amazement that first Monday morning as their brothers from North America began to unpack power drills, circular saws, transits, levels, picks, and shovels. Within thirty minutes some were busy clearing the lot, driving corner stakes, running building lines, and digging trenches for footings. The men rebuilt the church within a few days. Fresh teams arrived from the States and moved on to the next church.

The Body of Christ was proving that Christianity is not the exclusive faith of a few, but a worldwide fellowship of brothers and sisters who have bowed at Calvary, and who with Paul have said, "Lord, what wilt thou have me to do?"

Those who couldn't help on-site promptly sent $80,000 to provide emergency help, such as tents and blankets, then boosted that figure to $300,000. The Guatemalan experience firmed up the groundwork for later projects in other nations. For this kind of initiative over the years, the National Association of Evangelicals in 1979 named Walt Meloon its "Man of the Year."

In 1959, Walt Meloon toured Ecuador with Cameron Townsend, legendary founder of Wycliffe Bible Translators.

Several years earlier Auca Indians had murdered five American missionaries in the Ecuadorian jungle. Newspaper headlines carried news of the tragedy, and *Life* magazine sent its prize-winning photographer, Cornell Capa, to the scene. Other missionaries, including widows of the slain men, carried on the work until the very men who had murdered the American missionaries became Christians and turned from war to peace.

Such is the power of the gospel, but it could not have happened without the cooperation of Dayuma, an Auca woman who helped the missionaries translate the Scriptures into the Auca tongue. In July 1959, at the Wycliffe guest house in Quito, Ecuador, Walt Meloon presented Dayuma with a special gift from Correct Craft: a boat to use on the rivers of the Ecuadorian jungles to reach tribes with the gospel. Although originally built as an assault boat for the Vietnamese War, it had been rejected by the U.S. Army because it was six pounds overweight.

God continued to use the Meloons in this part of the world when, in September 1965, Chief Tariri, once Peru's most feared headhunter, visited Orlando and Correct Craft. A Delta jetliner brought him to Orlando, following a call Walt received from Texas oilman H. L. Hunt. Hunt told Walt that Chief Tariri wanted to visit a boat manufacturing plant, and Correct Craft had been selected. The firm hustled to give him an unforgettable welcome.

The mayor, the sheriff, Delta Airline's Orlando manager, prominent business and professional men, TV and news photographers, radio, press, and interested citizens turned out to greet him. Chief Tariri and his party, including Peruvian and Wycliffe officials and a news magazine photographer were the last out. A stewardess stepped off the plane carrying a gun case for the Chief, but no one was worried. The former assailant was a changed man.

What had happened to him?

The story goes back to two young women linguists of the Wycliffe Bible Translators and its scientific affiliate, the Summer Institute of Linguistics. In July 1950, Lorrie Anderson and Doris Cox arrived in the northern Peruvian jungles by airplane. Their mission was to establish contact with the Shapra tribe, near the Amazon River.

A Peruvian rubber-trader friend of Chief Tariri accompanied the girls and explained that they had come to tell the Shapras about God. The Indians believed it was a hoax and suspected the women were sent ahead by foreign men who would arrive later to murder them. But the girls themselves appeared harmless and, the tribe reasoned, they might be looking for husbands. (The girls would have been killed, tribesmen told them later, had they been men.)

"I hated the white men and stood ready to kill any who might come to my domain," Tariri later said in a book he dictated for Harper & Row publishers. "I was Ruler of the Seven Rivers," said the Chief. Tariri had led more successful war parties than any other chief in Peru's jungles. He and other tribesmen exchanged "recipes" on headshrinking.

Cautiously, the Shapras finally accepted the women and tried to help them learn their language. Tariri himself helped them translate the Scriptures into the Shapra dialect. In the process he was converted.

An immediate change came over his life. He began to preach within his own tribe and to other chiefs, urging them to stop their warfare. One tried to kill him. Tariri encouraged young people to enter school. Witch doctors, young warriors, women, and children began to accept Christ. Tariri eventually spoke before Peruvian government officials in Lima and told how the work of two young women had transformed not only his own life, but the life-style of the entire tribe.

Once in Orlando, a motorcycle escort, blue lights flashing, took the chief from McCoy airport to the Correct Craft plant. Walt showed Tariri and his entourage Correct Craft's fiberglass boats in various stages of production. When they at last reached the large finishing room, Tariri looked over and saw a boat with "TARIRI" painted on the side in bold letters. Unable to read English, he didn't catch the significance.

"Some day," he said through an interpreter, and pointing to the craft, "I'm going to have a boat just like that one."

Walt broke the good news. It already *was* his boat.

"Chief Tariri," he said, "we praise the Lord for you, and we love the Christ you do; and because we do, we present you with this boat that will send you through the jungle faster. We give you this boat in the name of the Lord Jesus Christ."

Tariri gratefully accepted the boat and replied that he wanted to use it to bring the gospel to those of his people he could not reach by paddle. "This isn't the old chief any more," he explained, and he related some of his life before his conversion.

At a banquet that followed, Tariri was joined at the head table by the Orlando police chief and Lorrie Anderson, one of the missionaries who more than a decade earlier had helped start such a remarkable chain of events. Orlando sheriff Dave Starr presented the smiling Tariri with a badge and made him an honorary deputy.

The honors were not over. Days later, at the New York World's Fair, a Wycliffe pavilion displayed a one-hundred-foot-long mural dramatizing the chief's conversion to Christianity. On July 28, at the twilight Tower of Lights Ceremony, Chief Tariri flipped a switch that turned on the most powerful light in the world. It was symbolic, announced Wycliffe founder Cameron Townsend, "of the enlightenment to once-forgotten tribes through bilingual education and by giving them, in their own exotic tongues, the greatest spiritual light in the world—the Bible."

That same year Correct Craft hosted Chief Ricardo Yaiguaje, his wife, and brother on their first visit to the United States from their Siona Indian tribe in Colombia. The Meloons escorted them to Cypress Gardens, where they presented them with a fiberglass Play'n'Ski boat. The chief thanked them profusely for "the fire canoe that flies." Ricardo jokingly suggested the boat might be used for a bathtub, a modern convenience he had seen for the first time only three days earlier.

Latin America still figured prominently in the Meloons' testimony years later. In 1981, Ralph, on one of his frequent business trips to push export sales, traveled to Caracas, Venezula; Buenos Aires, Argentina; Santiago, Chili; Lima, Peru; and Bogota, Colombia. No jungle tribes were on his route, but he knew the highly civilized, educated, and affluent people he'd meet—many of them in the boating and water-ski industry—still needed Jesus Christ. Ralph missed few chances to share the gospel.

He loaded his luggage with small items he'd leave with missionary friends and other contacts along the way. Cheese. Peanut butter. Ski Nautique T-shirts, caps, stickers, patches. Bubble gum and Tootsie Rolls for the children.

But at the air terminal in Caracas, an attendant told him his luggage was overweight and charged him an extra $250. Inwardly, Ralph fumed. All the little handouts weren't worth that much. The girl at the gate rechecked the scales and read it as $175. That helped, but Ralph was still upset as he settled back in his seat. He decided to pray.

Suddenly, he realized the irony of his situation. The things in that bag were free. They were items he would pass out without charge to those along the way, despite the seemingly unreasonable cost to deliver them. So it is with salvation. It is a free gift. But it cost the Savior dearly to deliver it.

Another Latin America trip took him again to Venezuela, where he went out of his way to visit Elpedio Martinez, Jr., at one time Venezuela's number two ranked water-skier. Elpedio Sr., Ralph learned, had a brain tumor and had only a little time to live. He needed Jesus.

Ralph inadvertently packed his Bible into his luggage instead of his briefcase. At Caracas, the airline lost his luggage—and his Bible. At the Holiday Inn that night he found a bilingual Gideon Bible. Suddenly it hit him. It's just what he needed for his meeting with Elpedio Sr. For the first time he "stole" a Bible.

When Ralph later arrived to talk to Elpedio Sr., he discovered that Elpedio Sr. could speak little English. The bilingual translation was the key, as Ralph read to him in English, and the family read in Spanish from parallel columns. Elpedio Sr., father of one of Venezuela's top-ranking water-skiers, accepted the Lord that day, only days before his death.

It may never have happened had not the airline lost Ralph's luggage and Bible, forcing Ralph to use the bilingual translation, which in turn allowed Elpedio Sr., to grasp the gospel clearly in his native tongue.

The Meloon enthusiasm for the gospel, whether among the tribes or the culturally elite, is always compatible with the spirit of the apostle Paul, as he writes of his desire to visit the seat of the Roman Empire: "For I owe a great debt to you and to everyone else, both to civilized people and uncivilized alike; yes, to the educated and uneducated alike. So, to the fullest extent of my ability, I am ready to come also to you in Rome to preach God's Good News" (Romans 1:14-15).

16

In Europe and the Mideast

Ralph and his wife, Betty, were shooting the rapids of the Dunajec River in the Pieniny Mountains not far from the Czechoslovakian border. It was August 1986. They were in Poland for eleven days on just one segment of a demanding three-month business trip, despite Ralph's age of sixty-nine. In pursuit of international markets, he had skipped through Europe too many times to count, hitting the major boat shows each year, and often top European water-ski events. Internationally, he logged more than 100,000 miles a year. But this was his first time to visit the Eastern Block.

Ralph was attending a water-ski tournament as a guest of the Polish government. Participants were all from Socialist countries: Poland, Russia, Bulgaria, Czechoslovakia, East Germany, and North Korea.

"We have seen Russian skiers in tournaments outside of the eastern bloc nations," Ralph said, "but we could never talk to them. Only the interpreters were allowed to talk with us. Here in Poland we communicate with their team captain, trainer, and team."

When two days of rain dampened the tournament, the Polish government assigned a man to hold an umbrella over Ralph's head the entire time. They also gave him a special seat in the roof-protected judge's tower, but he chose instead to roam among the skiers, parents, and onlookers sheltered in campers and tents below. With the help of two translators, he chatted with people in the crowd and passed out literally hundreds of business cards. A slick, one-fold card with a colorful Ski Nautique in action on the cover, it read:

> It has been a pleasure meeting you. May I share with you a little about our company and myself?
>
> My father began building boats more than 50 years ago. We are one of the oldest family owned boat manufacturing companies in the United States. We believe we manufacture one of the finest lines of recreational boats with inboard engines. They are owned and enjoyed by several kings and rulers of various nations. Correct Craft boats are used as Official Water Ski Tow Boats in more than 80 percent of the Water Ski Tournaments around the world.
>
> Every one of our boats starts in a master mold. The craftsmen know how to put it all together and the raw material soon turns out to be another quality boat.
>
> As a young man I discovered from the Bible that there is a Master Builder, God Himself. He can take a man's life, no matter how rough it seems to be, and create a new life which will be beautiful and useful. Life has been worth living since I asked Jesus Christ to become the Master Builder of my life and to recreate in me a new life which would be pleasing to Him.
>
> He will do the same for you if you ask Him. Please write me if I can be a help to you.
>
> > Sincerely,
> > Ralph Meloon, Sr.

Probably no executives distribute more business cards than do Ralph and Walt. The card serves as both a tract and conversation-starter. Almost everyone they meet, in the U.S. or abroad, receives one.

On Sunday morning, Ralph and Betty worshiped at the Baptist Church of Katowice. In Poland, services run two hours. Ralph, along with other guests, was a speaker. He told the congregation the story of his company, including its struggle with bankruptcy while making three thousand boats for the Vietnam War.

Later when a man asked him how a Christian could build boats for a war in Vietnam, Ralph responded that the United States has helped to keep people free all over the world.

"That's why our company built boats in World War II, to help free Poland from Hitler's domination," he explained.

The man seemed to understand.

Others told him they didn't like how capitalists run a country. Ralph shifted the focus from the economic issue to the sin of man. "That's where the real problem lies," he said.

It had taken this church, he learned, seventy years to complete its building. Three times the church had gathered the money for it, and three times it was taken away. The first time was by Adolph Hitler.

Back in their hotel room, one they were told was bugged, Ralph and Betty prayed and wept for a country that has not known true freedom for centuries.

The Polish government invited him back for another water-ski tournament in July 1987. Again Ralph understood a little more clearly the meaning of his life and the firm he helps direct. God surely foresaw this unusual Christian access to Poland and other lands when his dad helped make waterskiing a sport, and when Ralph trusted his life to the Lord a short time later. The two events, seemingly unrelated at the time, now made sense.

In January 1985, during one of the worst freezes ever in southern Europe, I joined Ralph, co-chairman of the board of Correct Craft, in London on one of his many European business trips.

Our first evening there a friend of Ralph's, who distributes Gideon Bibles, took us to a cottage prayer meeting ten minutes from Heathrow airport. It was the first of three prayer meetings we would attend in one week. The weather outside was cold, but the warmth of the Christian fellowship inside was unforgettable. Ralph had met with these people before. The small group found amusement in the fact that their special boatbuilding guest was accompanied by a man whose name happened to be "Flood." The chuckles turn to roaring laughter when the group leader announced that, entirely by coincidence, our Bible study that night would be the Genesis 6 account of Noah's flood!

The next morning we had breakfast with our hotel's assistant manager, who extended the invitation to make up for an earlier mix-up in Ralph's lodging arrangements. The gracious young lady apologized, but it was another opportunity to share the Correct Craft story and the gospel, this time with an executive of one of Europe's largest hotel chains.

We checked in at the boat show at Earls Court, where the building that once packed in crowds for a Billy Graham Crusade now glistened with its own indoor lake, with replica shops around its perimeters. Professional skiers staged mini-exhibitions there, though it was dangerous because of the tight quarters. Boats crowded the hall as far as you could see.

Although Ralph was busy at the Correct Craft exhibit, he took time to introduce me to special acquaintances, including Belgium's top water-skier. In talking with these people I could see the impact of the Meloons, even among those who did not necessarily share the family's strong religious convictions.

"They may not always understand us," Ralph told me later, "but they respect us."

Back in our hotel room, Ralph had an appointment with John Arkell, British Isles director of Campus Crusade, who briefed him on a major Christian event scheduled for the National Exhibition Center in Birmingham to follow up Billy Graham's Mission England, where fifty thousand people made commitments to Jesus Christ.

That night a Lebanese exporter and his wife picked us up for dinner in a Rolls Royce. Ralph's month-long circuit of boat shows would later take him to Beirut, and our genial host, Sany Nahas, expressed concern for Ralph's safety while there.

From London we left for the beautiful Isle of Wight, in the English Channel, boarding the ferry at Portsmouth.

"The Meloons once lived here," he explained, pointing to the shoreline, "before they migrated to America." Emigrants even transported the name of their city to the shores of New England—Portsmouth, New Hampshire. Both are boatbuilding cities by the sea.

Our ferry pulled into a beautiful inlet on the Isle of Wight. It was dark. Baptist Pastor Richard Steele, our escort, suddenly called our attention to lights flashing on and off from a home on the wooded hillside to our right. "That's Marge," he explained. "She's acknowledging our arrival." Within minutes we were relaxing in the lovely home of Frank and Marjorie Noltingk, where we spent the next three days.

The Noltingks are believers—he a lawyer; she an active and articulate leader in the life of the island, whose population mushrooms in the summer from a heavy influx of tourists. Ralph had stayed here two years earlier, when he had also brought his granddaughter, Lisa, with him. He had spent two weeks on the island helping the Castlehold Baptist Church of Newport through a United States/England evangelistic "exchange" program sponsored by the Southern Baptist Convention. At first the congregation had been leery of what to expect from the more overt American believers. In church-state England, British evangelicals are more low-key. But God had blessed the effort with conversions, substantial church growth, and spiritual renewal. The next year the congregation would send thirteen of its own to South Carolina and Florida to reciprocate.

Spiritual excitement was still in the air. Billy Graham had visited the British Isles months earlier, and many agreed that the long spiritual decline of the country, which has only a 5 percent church attendance, had bottomed out. On the Isle of Wight itself, there was a special sense of God's moving. The Castlehold Baptist Church was crowded both Sunday morning and evening. Meanwhile, residents of the twenty-six-mile-long island spoke highly of the Christian work among three large prisons there. Ironically, the catalyst for this spiritual movement was Prison Fellowship, the American-based work founded by Charles Colson.

With the Noltingks as hosts, we visited converts from the mission two years earlier, and Ralph renewed old acquaintances. Together we shared our Christian testimonies in one of the island's largest public high schools. In the hour-long taxi ride from Portsmouth back to London, Ralph shared his faith with our driver. He pressed the gospel for a bit, then changed the subject, but eventually came back to it. The driver seemed moved by what he heard.

The next day we left for Paris and another boat show. We landed only hours after an ice storm—and the temperature was a record three below. Bogged down in unprecedented mountain snows, the Ski Nautique that Ralph had ordered trucked from the French Riviera to Paris never made it to the show.

Following the boat show in Paris, I returned home. Ralph continued on for another two weeks, first to Dusseldorf, Germany, site of the world's largest boat show, then to Beirut.

Although no one knew it, a Trans World Airlines hostage crisis lay just around the corner. Meanwhile, a Middle East Airlines plane arrived from Frankfurt, Germany, with Ralph aboard. The city was tense. Ralph emerged from the plane. As he hit the bottom step of the ramp, he was suddenly grabbed and thrust into the backseat of a black limousine, surrounded by Lebanese soldiers. Quickly they escorted him to the terminal. For a few minutes Ralph was sure he had been kidnapped.

But Elecco Shiha, Correct Craft's importer in Lebanon, had made the arrangements to protect him. Most kidnapping in West Beirut happens at the airport, and an American business executive is always a prime target.

Despite the war atmosphere, much of the city conducted business as usual. Ski Nautiques, Martiniques, South Winds, and other Correct Craft boats dominated the yacht harbor. Construction was everywhere. Raymond, a Christian flight attendant Ralph met on the plane from Dusseldorf, invited Ralph to his home and church in Beirut's most dangerous neighborhood. Another Christian friend, Alecco, concerned about safety, arranged for a taxi to pick up Ralph at 6:45 P.M. Soon the taxi was making its way in driving rain through Syrian-held territory controlled by communist funding. Once held by the Palestine Liberation Organization (PLO), it had been heavily bombed.

As the taxi arrived at Raymond's home, suddenly the power went off in that district of the city. Through a window out the back corner, Raymond pointed to an apartment with a light powered by generator. It belonged to the neighborhood's communist leader, he explained. The atmosphere was eerie; Ralph felt uneasy.

It was time for prayer meeting. The men walked out the back, climbed over a pile of debris, and headed for a Baptist church a block away. Soon a small crowd of about forty-five gathered. Ralph gave his testimony. His translator, a man strong in spiritual conviction, was the president of Beirut's largest travel agency. Another in the crowd was principal of a Baptist school with nine hundred students, serving many of the homes and families in this war-torn sector. The dedication of this Christian group in such dismal setting, and the joy of their Christian fellowship left Ralph in tears. He has lasting memories of that time.

Finally one of the brethren warned, "If you don't go now, you may not get out tonight." The taxi roared off through narrow streets and traffic, returning Ralph to his friend Alecco, who was ready to call upon the army to rescue his American guest if he did not return by sundown.

Five hours later nine shells fell into the eastern sector only a short distance from where Ralph had crossed the "green line." Two children were killed.

17

In Frontier Alaska

A Super Cub on skis droned through the rugged Alaska Range southwest of Anchorage. In was late February 1986, and the temperature at ground level was twenty degrees below zero. At the controls was Ralph Jr., president of Pacific Coast Correct Craft, based in Soldotna near Anchorage. His father, Ralph Sr., rode in the back seat.

To their left they could see Illiamna Volcano. Beyond in the distance rose Augustine Volcano, which only a few weeks later would belch steam and ash nine miles into the air, disrupting ship and airline traffic throughout southcentral Alaska. Alex Russell, a medical doctor, flew his own Super Cub àlongside father and son; Alaskan flyers know it is always best to travel in pairs.

The two planes ranged through mountain peaks for more than two hours, en route to the caribou grounds. They landed on a remote lake near one of the larger herds and unloaded much of their gear, but they left their survival kits aboard. Alex stayed to tend camp. Father and son took off again into the mountains, this time destined for Port Alsworth, on Lake Clark, only a short distance from Twin Lakes, where author Dick Pronneke had penned perhaps Alaska's best seller, *One Man's Wilderness.*

The attraction in Port Alsworth was not caribou, but an unusual village whose inhabitants are all evangelical Christians.

On a lake of ice two-feet deep, the Super Cub taxied up to the home of Glenn and Patty Alsworth. Glenn is a son of the town's founder, Babe Alsworth. He was on a trip across the lake, but Patty warmly welcomed the party.

Barely one hundred populate Port Alsworth in the winter, but the town enjoys a $2 million dollar school, a small saw mill, two airstrips, and a post office, with air delivery three times a week. Glenn and Patty's home houses the town's telephone switchboard.

Townspeople gathered to greet the Meloons, who found the Christian fellowship here "a little bit of heaven." No one here has insurance; they can't buy it. If a house burns down, the townspeople simply rebuild it. When a little girl in the village had to be flown to Anchorage for a serious illness, medical bills mounted to $10,000. The people of Port Alsworth helped pay.

For three weeks each summer—and Alaska's summers indeed are short—Port Alsworth comes alive as a mission station. Natives and whites come from miles around for Christian camp. Many find the Savior. The town also reaches out to the heavy influx of sportsmen who pour into the village in summer, often boarding in the homes of Christians.

On this particular trip Ralph, Jr., left his dad to share his testimony with hospitable friends at Port Alsworth and flew back into caribou country to camp and hunt with Dr. Russell. The men returned with two nice caribou cleaned and packed aboard the plane. With no fuel to spare, son Ralph picked up his dad and returned through the mountains to Soldotna.

West Coast Correct Craft, a consumer-oriented arm of the West Coast market under Ralph Jr.'s direction, has its corporate offices in California. But for Ralph Jr., Alaska is home. His family has moved up to Soldotna to occupy a comfortable, rustic home on the banks of the Kenai River, waterway of the largest strain of king salmon worldwide. As a boat distributor, avid outdoorsman, flyer, and Christian philanthropist, this is the land he loves.

The night after their return from Fort Alsworth, the Meloon father and son found themselves among scores of Alaskan teenagers packed into the Kenai Peninsula's largest inn. It was the first banquet of the Kenai Youth For Christ movement, which Ralph Jr. helped organize. It was the largest single banquet ever held on the peninsula.

In July the Kenai Peninsula held its first water-ski camp, started by the Meloons in cooperation with Youth For Christ. It was advertised on local radio and TV. Christian skiers flew in from Orlando for the week-long exhibition and training camp. Hundreds of teenagers participated, and hundreds more of Kenai's residents turned out to watch. Skiers gave their testimonies, and a medical doctor preached. In the unusual outdoor setting, many heard the gospel for the first time and began to listen.

In September I flew to Soldotna to spend three days with Ralph Jr. and his family. We had planned a flight into the mountains, but Ralph Jr. left suddenly that morning with missionary pilots to help rescue a friend whose plane had gone down on a gravel bar in difficult mountain terrain. Word soon arrived that the rescue party was weathered in for at least one day, maybe two.

At his home on the Kenai River, the family extended its gracious hospitality. In the living room, two Alaskan Dall sheep, a mountain goat, and a caribou stared down at me—all among Ralph Jr.'s trophies. Two young nephews, the oldest six, showed me through "Uncle Ralph's" basement gun shop. Like old hunting pros, they walked me through the process of how their uncle makes bullets. Tanya Meloon, Ralph Jr.'s vivacious high school daughter, told me enthusiastically about her plans to enroll at Master's College in southern California, headed by Dr. John

MacArthur. Her sister Lisa was already enrolled at Wheaton College in Illinois.

By the second day the bad mountain weather had moved into the Kenai peninsula, making the men's return even more uncertain.

Ralph's family told me he is knowledgeable about computers, and for several months he had been installing a system for the Missionary Aviation and Repair Center (MARC), a mile away. Founded in 1964 by one-time Nome pastor Roald Amundsen, MARC has long been the aerial service upon which much of the missionary work in Alaska relies. Ralph Jr. flies his Super Cub with them when he can and has sold them a twin engine plane of his own at a good price. His plans to escort me through the operation had been disrupted by his stranded situation.

Suddenly the letterhead on some mail lying by Ralph Jr.'s home computer caught my attention. The name on the letterhead was the same as that of a Christian friend of mine from army days at Fort Lewis, Washington, whom I had not seen for twenty-one years (we'd once sung together in a Fort Lewis quartet, and I had ushered at his Idaho wedding). Until that moment I hadn't even known his whereabouts! I checked the Soldotna telephone directory and called Chuck Obendorf, Ralph Jr.'s certified public accountant. Within minutes he and his wife were at the door to take me to lunch. This surprise reunion was no coincidence.

"Since Ralph is still hung up in the mountains," Chuck said, "I'll introduce you to all the folk over at MARC."

We arrived at the MARC hangar, only yards from the Soldotna air terminal where I had landed the evening before. Roald Amundsen, the legendary MARC founder, stepped out of the plane that had just landed.

"Augustine is throwing dust again," he said. That meant planes should stay out of range; their engines couldn't swallow it.

I met Roald Amundsen, who soon had us looking at a large Alaskan map on the wall inside the center.

"We're looking at a state more than twice the size of Texas," he explained. "Yet there are virtually no roads in the western part of the state. Only the rivers and trails left by snowmobiles and dog teams."

In years past missionaries had to travel for days by dog sled, often in sub-zero temperatures, to reach remote villages. Today MARC pilots safely fly those same miles over snow-covered tundra and through rugged mountain ranges in a fraction of the time.

They are piloted by men like Fred Chambers, recently retired as a senior pilot of 747s for American Airlines. Although now over seventy, he still makes four to six parachute jumps a year.[1]

They are men like Dick Page, a graduate of Moody Bible Institute's missionary aviation school, which has trained more than half the world's missionary pilots. Dave Cochran, on loan from Arctic Missions, and Bob Widman, are among them.

Since MARC began, its pilots have safely flown nearly 3 million miles. In his own flying career (which predates MARC) as a pastor and pilot for Evangelical Covenant Missions, Roald Amundsen has probably flown nearly a million miles.

What do these pilots carry? Missionaries, generators, natives, medical supplies, children, food, young people, camp counselors, sick people, athletic teams, schoolteachers. The list is endless.

From his twenty years' experience as a pastor in Nome, Roald will tell you that it's almost impossible to be both a good pastor and a good pilot. "You either let the church slide, or your flying deteriorates. That's why we launched MARC."

1. Fred Chambers also plays an airline pilot in an Alaskan film drama called *Tough Men* (Gospel Films).

"Where do you see the greatest spiritual results to-day?" I asked.

"In the summer Bible camps. Many become Christians. And in those churches out there where the pastor has been sticking it out for years."

In Alaska, small planes jam some village airports like autos in the parking lot of a shopping mall. But flying over Alaskan terrain can be risky—especially for the in-experienced. Crashes frequently occur.

By the next day Ralph Jr. was back from the mountains, having first picked up his wife, Carolyn, who landed in Anchorage at midnight on a flight from California. He relaxed on the sofa in his living room and told us about his weekend.

"We were flying into Merrill Pass. I was following the plane ahead of me. I kept coming down in elevation to keep below the cloud ceiling. The dangerous dogleg of the pass was just ahead. You have only seconds to turn around if it's not clear. It was clear enough to go through, but not by much. The pass below is like a junkyard. All kinds of planes down there," he said.

Although an experienced pilot in high performance singles and twins, Ralph Jr. had barely learned to fly the standard Alaska bush plane, a tail dragger, when he bought several in California, flew them one by one to Alaska, then sold them, making each return flight by commercial jet.

The trips were a far cry from his first one to Alaska. He was a teenager in 1959 when the family drove the Al-can Highway, with no paved roads for more than a thousand miles. Storms had washed out a bridge at Peace River in British Columbia. Only a railroad trestle re-mained. Placing boards on the rails, their car followed others one hundred feet apart as they made the perilous crossing over a deep ravine.

In the Yukon, Ralph Jr. befriended a drunken Indi-an, playfully shoved him, then ran for the car as the man chased him. The lad managed to reach the car and lock himself in. His mother wrote a postcard home with the disturbing message: "A drunk Indian is trying to get into the car."

That was the last message the family in Orlando received for two weeks. By that time, convinced that some disaster had befallen the travelers, the family had dispatched Walt to Alaska to conduct a search. The Meloons called an all-night prayer meeting. That very night, Ralph Sr. felt compelled to call home. He was shocked to learn that his dad, usually optimistic, had given up the party for dead, and had even already informed his oldest married daughter of the tragedy!

In spite of such family adventures, Ralph Jr. now believes Alaska is his call. His dad sometimes worries that the business suffers a bit, but Ralph Jr. says, "As much as I like it, I don't want the business to run my life." He is quick to give credit, however, to his hard-working brother, Ken, who directs Midwest Correct Craft and Southwest Correct Craft.

As Ralph Jr. blends business with the outdoors, few know his expertise with languages. He majored in biblical studies at Bob Jones University, with minors in Greek and speech. Then, after several terms at Gordon Divinity School and Winona Lake Summer School of Theology, he went to Wheaton Graduate School of Theology, where he majored in Greek and minored in Hebrew with an A average. Subsequently, he was accepted by the Department of Hebrew and Semitic studies at the University of Wisconsin and briefly pursued a Ph.D. with a major in Hebrew and a minor in classical Greek. It was during this period that Ralph Jr. felt called to re-enter the boat business of which he was so much a part.

The family worships at fast-growing Soldotna Bible Chapel, pastored by a one-time Montana rancher. Ralph Jr. seems to have a natural rapport with the young generation of Alaskans who flock around him after church to hear him relate, in best storytelling form, his latest wilderness escapades.

In fact, Ralph Jr. has begun to pursue his imaginative dreams for a remote Christian retreat site beyond the Alaska Range in what may well be the wildest part of Alaska. Given his adventurous pioneer spirit and ingenuities, it just might happen.

18

In China and the Far East: Boats Open the Door

In 1949, under revolutionary leader Mao Tse-tung, Socialists took control of mainland China. They expelled foreign missionaries and turned churches into warehouses and museums. They confiscated Bibles. An estimated 4 million Christians were forced to meet in secret, if they met at all. The Socialist regime assumed those believers would either abandon their faith or eventually die off, and the church disappear.

Doors remained shut to the outside world for more than a quarter century. After years of scanty information, many wondered if the church had been destroyed. Were all the years of sacrificial pioneer work by missionaries such as Hudson Taylor, Eric Liddell, and a parade of others totally wasted?

Years passed. Then a crack finally opened in the Bamboo Curtain. A few reports began to filter out. Then more. The real story unfolded. The church was not gone; it was greater than ever—some reports said up to 50 million—despite the Socialist attempt to stamp it out. Few church buildings existed, but there were tens of thousands of small house churches where believers met for prayer, Bible study, and worship. The church of Jesus Christ lived on!

As the door to the West reopened, Walt received an invitation from the People's Republic of China. It came through the Christian and Missionary Alliance church, which had planted churches there before the revolution. He was invited to help search for any of the former Christian and Missionary Alliance church buildings that may have survived. Chinese officials even offered to help restore them. Walt and some associates made the trip. They found no Christian and Missionary Alliance churches, but uncovered what was once a Southern Baptist church.

Meanwhile, Walt took Bibles with him for the heads of China's Water Ski Federation, each engraved with the recipient's name. John Bechtel of the Arthur S. DeMoss Foundation helped set it up. Bechtel was born in China of missionary parents. His family had been forced out by the Socialists. Bechtel knew the language well and had already engineered the entrance of Christian basketball teams into this land.

China's water-ski officials received the party warmly. The sport—even the water-ski association itself—was new there. The delegation was honored at banquets and receptions. Upon leaving, Walt invited the People's Republic of China to send a water-ski delegation to the United States as guests of Correct Craft. They accepted.

Three Chinese guests arrived in Orlando: a skier, a coach, and an interpreter. They spent two weeks at Bill Peterson's Ski School in Windermer, Florida, where Xiang Qinhai learned how to jump and worked on improving his slalom and trick skiing skills. Between workouts they visited the major tourist sites. Before their return, they were presented personalized Bibles.

In July 1985, Correct Craft hosted two officials of the China Sports Service—one of them in charge of all water sports in China. Their nation's first major water-ski tournament was imminent, so they came specifically to watch the famed Masters tournament at Callaway Gardens. They spent the last four days of their visit at Camp-of-the-Woods in the New York Adirondacks.

The doors continued to open. Walt returned to the People's Republic of China. So did Ralph, with Correct Craft engineer Bill Snook. Together they conducted seminars on how to use and maintain the Ski Nautique 2001, which China had selected to pull its water-ski teams. Ralph requested that Sunday be left open so he could attend church, which turned out to be a Cantonese-speaking evangelical congregation. The next Sunday at another church, they found Baptist hymnals in the pews. Later their interpreter asked many questions about the sermon. He had never heard about Jesus Christ.

A few years earlier in July 1980, Ralph joined a two-week mission with the Southern Baptists in Seoul and Inchon, despite a sudden economic recession in the States that threw Correct Craft into a momentary cash flow crisis. He considered canceling but decided to go. Besides, he had already arranged to take along his seventeen-year-old grandson, Eric Abel.

They flew through Tokyo to touch base with officials of the Japanese Water Ski Federation, then proceeded to Seoul. At the airport Ralph engaged a young lady in a conversation about spiritual matters. She was a U.S. Army sergeant from Indiana. Before leaving the airport, she made a clear decision for Jesus.

In Korea, the West has no monopoly on Christianity. Instead, Koreans set the pace. Hundreds of thousands rise in the early morning for prayer. In Seoul is located the largest church congregation in the world, now numbering more than one half million members, far greater than any congregation in the United States. Its pastoral staff alone numbers in the thousands. On Sunday, worship services run back to back throughout the day. In no other nation has Christianity exploded as it has in Korea in the twentieth century.

When Ralph and Eric checked into Korea's largest hotel, a message awaited them from Chung Se Young,

president of the nation's largest automobile manufacturer and head of Korea's water-ski federation. He and top
water-skiers awaited them on an upper floor for lunch.
On a strict diet from recent illness, Ralph declined the
fine meats offered and asked for dry cereal. He requested corn flakes, but the waiter didn't understand. Eventually a cook produced a box of corn flakes from the
kitchen. Ralph clipped the top of the box and thereafter
simply flashed the boxtop to waiters.

For nearly two weeks Ralph and his grandson, coop-
erating in a special evangelism outreach, walked miles
through Seoul each day with other believers, both Korean and American, sharing the gospel. They found warm
hospitality everywhere, and much spiritual response.
Each time another person accepted Jesus as his Savior,
fellow Korean Christians joyfully clapped their hands. To
share the good news they rose early, skipped lunch, and
pursued souls into the late evening.

On their only day off, a Korean general escorted
Ralph and his grandson into an "intercept" tunnel near
the border with Communist North Korea. It had been
built by North Koreans to infiltrate South Korea with
thousands of the enemy. But listening devices now detect
their drilling operations, and when the cutting starts,
South Koreans are soon there to stop it.

Ralph and his grandson walked into one of these intercept tunnels for several miles, until they came face to
face with North Korean guns inside the mountain. It was
obviously time to turn back.

As in the Christian life, which the Bible describes as
a "spiritual warfare," the enemy seldom backs off. Many
Koreans know both the spiritual freedoms of their faith
and the near presence of the enemy.

In January of 1969 Walt left on a nine-week tour
with the Billy Graham Evangelistic team, which took him

through Honolulu, Kuala Lumpur in Malaysia, Bali, Indonesia, Singapore, Australia, and New Zealand.

The Meloons' involvement with missions in Indonesia dates back at least a quarter century. In 1955 Correct Craft gave missionaries Bob and Doris Fraser a fifteen thousand dollar houseboat at half price. Customized for the Fraser's at the old Titusville plant, it became their home for seven years as they served eleven mission stations on the south coast of West Irian.

Later in 1969 Wycliffe missionary Marilyn Laszlo, whose remarkable tribal work in Papua New Guinea inspired the film "River of Light," received a sixteen-foot boat from Correct Craft. For years she had traveled up and down the majestic Sepik River by dugout canoe. The 110-mile trip took a grueling ten to twelve hours. She and her companions often were sick the following day from the hot sun. Now the trip would take only four hours. Later she wrote, "What an impact this has had on the Sepik tribe. The people here in the village of Hauna where I live just could not imagine someone giving a gift like that."

In 1977, Walt embarked on a five-week venture to the Far East, including the Philippines, Hong Kong, and Taiwan on behalf of the Alliance Men (of the Christian and Missionary Alliance church) and the Billy Graham Evangelistic association. Associate evangelist Grady Wilson headed the team. Walt spoke up to three times a day. He spent most of the time in the Philippines, where he addressed the downtown Manila Kiwanis Club, among other engagements. His itinerary culminated in November with a major Billy Graham Crusade in the Philippines, during which he shared his testimony in Graham's School of Evangelism.

But this was not Walt's first trip to the Philippines; he had been there before, on behalf of the Alliance Men.

One of those men, Jun Vencer, later became the general secretary of the Philippine Council of Evangelical Churches. He has also called Walt "one of the most influential men upon my life."

Walt fell in love with the country and its people. "When we get to heaven," he says, "the smiling Filipinos are surely going to be in charge of hospitality!"

On this trip in 1977 he made another observation: "The city of Manila—and all of the Philippines—is open. There will be no stopping the irresistible working of God's Holy Spirit as He builds His church in the hearts of the people."

Nine years later, in 1986, political storm clouds gathered over this Far East nation, as evidence grew of wide-scale corruption in the regime of President Ferdinand Marcos. Traveling in the Philippines at the time, Ralph observed the tension. When he traveled in the southern part of the islands the government assigned him an armed guard.

"This was a mistake," he said later. "I shouldn't have allowed it. I would have been better off not to have had anybody who represented President Marcos around me, because this is who the revolutionaries were after."

Before Ralph and his wife, Betty, left the islands, an earthquake shook their hotel in Bargio. Betty was asleep, but Ralph had stayed up to pray. The earthquake registered 5.5 on the Richter scale. It threw Ralph to the floor as he tried to make his way to the hallway door. Hotel guests ran up and down the halls alerting occupants. But no one was hurt.

Ralph later quipped to his wife, "I didn't know my prayers could make the whole hotel shake."

But before long, prayer would shake the Philippines.

In early 1986, Ferdinand Marcos still refused to step down, and political crisis grew. Widespread bloodshed seemed inevitable, and the free world feared that the

Philippines would be lost to Communism in the inevitable turmoil. Out of the chaos came Corazon Aquino, who took charge in the hour of crisis.

Meanwhile, hundreds of thousands of Christians, both Protestant and Catholic, united in prayer—not just privately, but in the streets, and the nation avoided a disaster. Even much of the Philippine public acknowledged that such a turn of events must have been "a work of God." Corazon Aquino and her ambassador to the United States (formerly director of the Philippine Bible Society) urged that the Scriptures be put into the hands of her nation on a mass scale.[1]

The future of the Philippines remains uncertain, and the record of Mrs. Aquino's regime might be viewed by some as "mixed." But seasoned Christian businessmen like Walt and Ralph are firmly convinced that, as in the history of America, the gospel does indeed prosper both people and nations who respond to it. "Blessed is the nation whose God is the Lord" (Psalm 33:12).

That is why these men have never been content simply to build boats or run the family business. They have always felt compelled to "be about their Father's business."

And because of this conviction, they have left an imprint upon the world of business ethics, upon the water-ski world, and upon those who shape the destinies of nations.

---

1. Mrs. Aquino's husband, Benigno, assassinated in August 1983 when he stepped off an airplane at Manila, had become an evangelical Christian while a political prisoner. The book that changed his life: *Born Again*, by Charles Colson.

Appendix A
Correct Craft Corporate Milestones

1925   W. C. Meloon founds the Florida Variety Boat Company, locating the first plant in Pine Castle, Florida. The product line: outboard racing boats, rowboats, and a few sailboats.

1930   The plant becomes known as the Pine Castle Boat and Construction Company.

1938   W.C. changes the name of the product to Correct Craft after hearing a radio commercial extolling the virtues of "the correct heel for your shoe." *Great,* he thought, *why not "the correct craft for you"?*

1942   Another plant is built in Titusville to manufacture boats for government contracts for the war effort. Soon after, large cruisers are added to the production schedule.

1945   Production of plywood boats begins.

1948   Production for first complete mahogany inboards, nineteen-foot racing runabouts, and custom-designed runabouts begins.

1950   First *Orlando Tribune* magazine is published. The editor: Norman M. Sewell.

1952   Banner year—one of the biggest years of
            sales and production in the history of Correct
            Craft.

1958   Production ends on the last of the true run-
            abouts—the eighteen-foot Collegian.

1960   Titusville plant closes; era of the large cruiser
            ends.

1961   Beginning of the fiberglass era. The first Ski
            Nautique built with a whopping price tag of
            $4,500, including the trailer.

1966-1979   Correct Craft introduces a multitude of new
            boat designs: the 24' deep-V San Juan, the
            Mustang, the Martinique line, the 20' and 23'
            Fish Nautiques. The 21' Cuddy Cabin was in-
            troduced and marked as the all around fam-
            ily boat. The 23' Cuddy began production.

1970   The Ski Nautique is redesigned.

1979   The growing interest in barefoot skiing
            brings about the ideal boat for the sport—the
            Barefoot Nautique. Correct Craft employs
            more than one hundred workers, including a
            complete remodeled and modern trailer fa-
            cility.

1982   The year of the 2001 Ski Nautique. Correct
            Craft introduces this superior boat, which re-
            mains the industry standard.

1983   The *Orlando Tribune* is changed to the *Cor-
            rect Craft Tribune* with a slick, full-color cover

and contemporary magazine design, and with Harvey McLeod as editor.

1985   Walter N. Meloon is promoted to president, making him the third generation to hold that title. The year marks the silver anniversary for the Ski Nautique, and a drawing for a free boat is a huge success. The winner is from Houston, Texas.

1987   The future looks bright, and the recreational boating industry is strong. Correct Craft's insistence on quality craftsmanship, materials, and production, combined with the inner strength provided by strong family ties and religious conviction, will always be the leading factors in the firm's success.

Appendix B
The Meloon Family Tree

Walter C. Meloon (1893-1974)
(founder of Correct Craft)
Marion (Hamm) Meloon (1892-1986)

Second Generation

Children of Walter C. and Marion Meloon:

Walter O. Meloon (1915)
(Secretary and Treasurer of the Board, Correct Craft)
Ralph C. Meloon, Sr. (1917)
(Chairman of the Board, Correct Craft)
Harold E. Meloon (1920)

Third Generation

Children of Walter O. and Ann Meloon:

Walter N. Meloon
(President, Correct Craft)
Etta Meloon Warner

Children of Ralph C. and Betty Meloon:

Ralph C. Meloon, Jr. (daughters Lisa and Tanya)
(President, Pacific Coast Correct Craft)
Ken Meloon
(President, Midwest Correct Craft)
Marion Meloon Abel

Children of Harold E. and Jewel Meloon

Shirley Meloon
Harold Meloon, Jr.
Daniel Meloon
Steve Meloon

Appendix C
Board of Directors of Correct Craft

Ralph C. Meloon, Sr., Chairman

Walter O. Meloon, Secretary and Treasurer

Russel J. Hovde, Retired from Continental Illinois Bank, Chicago

Torrey Mosvold, Retired from Mosvold Shipping Company, Norway

Norm Sonju, Chief Operating Officer and General Manager, Dallas Mavericks

Jim Welch, Attorney for Correct Craft

Gordon Purdy, Chairman, Camp-of-the-Woods, New York

Don Pennington, Former Vice President and Chief Financial Officer, Vassett, Walker, Inc., New York

David Chambers, Retired from Mid-Atlantic Correct Craft

Moody Press, a ministry of the Moody Bible Institute, is designed for education, evangelization, and edification. If we may assist you in knowing more about Christ and the Christian life, please write us without obligation: Moody Press, c/o MLM, Chicago, Illinois 60610.